INDUSTRY AND GOVERNMENT IN
FRANCE AND ENGLAND,
1540–1640

INDUSTRY AND GOVERNMENT IN FRANCE AND ENGLAND, 1540-1640

By JOHN U. NEF

Cornell Paperbacks

CORNELL UNIVERSITY PRESS

ITHACA AND LONDON

First published in the *Memoirs of the
American Philosophical Society,* vol. XV
(1940). Reprinted by permission.

CORNELL UNIVERSITY PRESS

First printing, Great Seal Books, 1957
Second printing, 1962
Third printing, Cornell Paperbacks, 1964
Fourth printing, 1967
Fifth printing, 1969

STANDARD BOOK NUMBER 8014-9053-7
PRINTED IN THE UNITED STATES OF AMERICA
BY VALLEY OFFSET, INC.

PREFACE

This essay, originally published in 1940, can stand by itself, I hope, as an inquiry into the interrelations between industrial and constitutional history during the hundred years or so following the Reformation. But I ought perhaps to call the reader's attention to other works of mine, which have appeared since that time and which help to reveal the general historical importance of that period for the genesis of the industrial civilization which now envelops the world. I have in mind especially *War and Human Progress* (Cambridge, Mass., 1950), part I; "The Genesis of Industrialism and Modern Science" in *Essays in Honor of Conyers Read* (ed. Norton Downs; Chicago, 1953), pp. 200–269; *La Naissance de la civilisation industrielle et le monde contemporain* (Paris, 1954); and *Cultural Foundations of Industrial Civilization* (Cambridge, 1957).

Today the freedom of economic enterprise and the individualism in conduct and in thought that accompanied the rise of industrialism are on trial. When guided by a love of truth and right, free enterprise and individualism are of very great benefit to mankind. When they become ends in themselves, independent of all other values, religious, ethical, and artistic, men lose the faith and the sense of responsibility which are essential to the survival of both free enterprise and individualism. Four centuries after the Reformation, the lines of Milton speak to us with a special meaning.

> He gave us onely over Beast, Fish, Fowl
> Dominion absolute; that right we hold
> By his donation; but Man over men
> He made not Lord; such title to himself
> Reserving, human left from human free.

*   *   *   *   *

> Yet sometimes Nations will decline so low
> From vertue, which is reason, that no wrong,
> But Justice, and some fatal curse annext
> Deprives them of thir outward libertie,
> Thir inward lost. . . .

The peoples who have inherited western civilization must regain their inward, if they are to retain their outward liberty. It would seem to be the duty of the scholar, dedicated to the search for truth, to help them, according to the means at his disposal, to re-establish the sense of proportion in the order of goods that they have been losing during the last half century. It would seem to be his duty to demonstrate again that, notwithstanding the teachings of many followers of Marx and Freud, there is a realm in which the human mind and spirit can work for good or evil, independently of material circumstances. The future of civilization depends upon the cultivation of this realm for good.

If the industrial historian is to help in guiding men into the ways of truth, justice, reason, and virtue, he should consider industrial history in relation to the whole of history, including the history of thought and of the arts. The disposition of historians during the last century to regard whatever small subject they have treated as independent of the rest of history has contributed to a confusion of means with ends. The relations of changes in the form of government to industrial development, and of industrial development to changes in the form of government, with which I am concerned in this essay, are obviously only aspects of the much larger subject of industry and civilization. But there is some justification for publishing a short separate treatise concerning the connections between the history of government and of industry. They have a special importance in our time, when some governments are abandoning all responsibility either to parliament or to the divine will of the Christian God. In the seventeenth century, in England and France, the responsibility of governments to the one or the other was established, and it became impossible in either country for a ruler to govern exclusively according to the precepts and the political philosophy of Machiavelli. Today that is no longer impossible. In order to understand why the responsibility of rulers to God or to a representative assembly is breaking down, it is necessary to understand how that responsibility was built up in early modern times. I hope this essay may contribute in a small way to such an understanding.

I was grateful for the opportunity offered me in 1940 by the American Philosophical Society to print the essay under its auspices. The essay appeared when the world was going to war, and, in the hustle and excitement of current events, its relevance to the deeper issues which set the stage for events was perhaps not fully recognized.

I take great pleasure in again expressing my obligations to several persons without whose support I should have hardly had the zest, under the stress of these events, to complete this work. My debts to my late wife, Elinor Castle Nef, who has left valuable contributions to American letters, are so great at all points, and especially in connection with chapter 3, that it would be impossible to enumerate them. My conversations with Robert Hutchins, then President of the University of Chicago, were of much value to me in interpreting the extensive original material I had gathered. My debts to Professor R. H. Tawney and to Professor Jacques Maritain are also heavy. Although Mr. Tawney did not read these pages, I had the advantage of talking over with him some of the problems with which they deal. Although they were written before I had heard the series of admirable lectures on the economic background of the English revolutions of the seventeenth century, which he gave at the University of Chicago during the Spring Quarter of 1939, I learned much from these lectures. Professor F. H. Knight read through two versions of this essay and made several helpful criticisms. Professor Chester W. Wright and my late mother-in-law, Mrs. M. W. Castle, also took trouble over it. To Professor Conyers Read, who had helped me constantly with my historical work since I sat at his feet as a college freshman, I owed my opportunity to publish under the auspices of the Philosophical Society. I need hardly add that none of these friends are responsible for any of the shortcomings of this essay, of which no one is more conscious than its author.

I am also indebted to my colleague and friend, Dean Robert Redfield, and to the Social Science Research Committee of the University of Chicago for providing me with the accurate and very helpful assistance of Miss Diane Greeter and Mrs. Margaret DeVinney. Miss Stella Lange, of St. Mary's College, Notre Dame, Indiana, gave me invaluable help in running down and checking references.

My work in the French archives was facilitated by the kindness of my friends, Monsieur Georges Bourgin and the late Georges Espinas, to both of whom I am very grateful. For copies of various documents which I used I am indebted to Monsieur Albert Morot and to Monsieur Jacques Monicat of the Archives Nationales, to Monsieur Raoul Busquet of Marseilles, to Messieurs de Dainville and Maury of Montpellier, to Monsieur Alibert of Toulouse and to Monsieur M. Courtecuisse of Draguignan. My greatest obligation for manuscript materials was to Professor F. J. Fisher. I do not know what I should have done without his help in the London archives. He made many transcripts and summaries of documents for me, work for which I had neither the time nor the inclination. I can never thank him adequately for his kindness.

JOHN U. NEF

Chicago, Illinois
April 17, 1957

TABLE OF CONTENTS

CHAPTER 1

INTRODUCTION

There have been two industrial revolutions in England, not one. The first occurred during the hundred years that followed the dissolution of the monasteries, in 1536 and 1539. This was not an age of rapid economic change in France. No industrial revolution occurred there to match the one taking place across the Channel. In the reign of Henry VIII, which ended in 1547, England had been industrially in a backwater compared with most continental countries, including France. During the next eighty years, the positions of the two countries were reversed as a result of a great industrial expansion which began in England in the forties of the sixteenth century and was most rapid between about 1575 and 1620. By the reign of Charles I, from 1625 to 1642, England was on the point of becoming, if she had not already become, the leading nation of Europe in mining and heavy manufacturing. In these industries the French were backward. In the reign of Louis XIII, from 1610 to 1643, France was producing very much less coal, copper and tin than England. She was producing very much less alum, a substance essential for dyeing cloth, at a time when the making of cloth employed more hands in both countries than any other industry. Relative to her population, France was producing less woolen cloth, less iron, glass and soap, less lime and fewer bricks for building. Costly labor-saving machinery, driven by horse or water power, was less widely used than in English industry; the scale of enterprise was smaller. In England there were already scores of mines and small factories in which more than a dozen laborers worked, and more than a thousand pounds sterling of capital were invested, a sum equivalent to perhaps four or five thousand pounds in the money of our own day. In France, with a population about three times as large as that of England, there were probably not a third as many of these mines and small factories. It was only in the making of luxury wares—such as lace, silks, and tapestries, and works of art modeled in glass, metal, clay, and stone—that the French had retained and increased the advantage they had always had over the English. Such wares found their market exclusively among the wealthy, and in France mainly among courtiers and great noblemen.[1]

How are we to account for the very different course of industrial development in France and England between 1540 and 1640? The explanation cannot be found in any one branch of history, such as religious, political, or financial history, or the history of science. All the main currents of historical development influenced industrial history in varying degrees, just as all the main currents of industrial history influenced in varying degrees every other aspect of historical development. An understanding of the nature of these influences and of their relative importance helps to make intelligible the course of European civilization since the Reformation. The relations between industrial and constitutional history provide one instructive chapter concerning the rise of capitalist industry and of representative government in western Europe.

The world into which my generation was born was a world in which government was carried on, in varying degrees and with varying success, with the consent of the governed. The sovereign authority, at least in Great Britain, France, the United States, many of the smaller states of Europe, and at the moment even Italy, rested not in a monarch, or a dictator, or an oligarchy, but in a representative assembly chosen by a vote of the people. We have lived to see the democratic principle of government, for which our ancestors fought, and which our fathers (some with the tears of satisfaction in their eyes) believed to be permanently established, placed on the defensive.

[1] J. U. Nef, "A Comparison of Industrial Growth in France and England from 1540 to 1640," in *Journal of Political Economy*, vol. xliv (1936), pp. 289–317, 505–33, 643–66; "Prices and Industrial Capitalism in France and England, 1540–1640," in *Economic History Review*, vol. vii (1937), pp. 159–62.

Whether the attack on representative government succeeds, or whether again, in President Wilson's fine phrase, the world is made "safe for democracy," our descendants centuries hence are likely to consider the establishment of democratic government, in states with populations running into tens of millions, as one of the remarkable achievements of western civilization.

Fustel de Coulanges, in his penetrating inquiry into Graeco-Roman civilization, argued that individualism and liberty in our western sense were unknown in classical times; that they are associated primarily with Christianity and with western civilization.[2] In the Middle Ages political authority was generally in the hands of autocrats. It was not until the nineteenth century that the principle of government with the consent of the governed gained the ascendency in the west. In the struggle during modern times for the establishment of this principle, England took the initiative and played the leading part, at least until the American and French revolutions. The course of English history between the death of Henry VIII, in 1547, and the execution of Charles I, in 1649, was of great, perhaps of decisive, importance in bringing the constitutional monarchy into being. The events of these hundred years culminated in the abolition of some of the most important administrative and judicial machinery for enforcing the royal will. Charles I's attempt to govern without parliament, and to levy taxes without the consent of the house of commons, cost him his head.

Meanwhile across the Channel the authority of the French crown, weakened temporarily during the religious wars which first broke out in 1560, was stronger than ever by the middle of the seventeenth century. The principle of the divine right of kings was universally acknowledged by writers on political theory. The states general met for the last time in 1614, not to be summoned again until 1789. The *parlements,* and especially the *parlement de Paris,* had greater powers in the late sixteenth and seventeenth centu-

[2] *La cité antique,* II, ch. x, no. 3.

ries than the states general, but these bodies were in no sense representative assemblies. Neither the *parlement de Paris* nor any of the provincial *parlements* represented, as the English parliament to some extent did, the interests of wealthy capitalists who had invested their fortunes in large-scale enterprises in trade and industry. The *parlement de Paris* was made up of a few great nobles and churchmen, together with the leading crown lawyers, holding office for life. Toward the end of Louis XIII's reign, in 1635, it had 120 members.[3] Its pretensions to a measure of independent sovereign authority during the minority of Louis XIV, and especially during the revolt of the Fronde from 1648 to 1653, were short-lived. When peace was re-established, it retained its ancient right to register the enactments of the crown and to exercise some legislative independence on matters not already covered by acts of the crown, pending the passage of such acts. But it was left without the initiative in political matters that it had aimed to acquire.[4] When he came of age, Louis XIV governed a larger territory more effectively and more absolutely than any of his predecessors.

The contrasts between the constitutional histories of England and France from 1540 to 1640 were as striking as the contrasts between their industrial histories. Was this accidental? Or were there connections between constitutional and industrial history which help to account for the contrasts in both?

Today representative government is on the defensive. One of the great problems of our time is how to save it, how to retain those principles connected with it that have been of benefit to man, and to discard those that have done him harm. It is important for all persons concerned with the future of western civilization to find out how representative government came into existence, and what its in-

[3] A. Chéruel, *Dictionnaire historique des institutions . . . de la France*, 8th ed., Paris, 1910, vol. ii, p. 945.

[4] Cf. A. Esmein, *Cours élémentaire d'histoire du droit français*, 15th ed., Paris, 1925, pp. 516, 518–19.

fluence on human welfare has been. In this essay, we are concerned with one segment of that problem, artificially cut off as all segments must be from the whole problem. How did government interference with economic life influence industrial development and general welfare in France and England in the sixteenth and early seventeenth centuries? How did industrial development influence the form of government? [5]

In trying to answer those questions we should know, first, whether the crown was already more powerful in France than in England at the beginning of the sixteenth century, when France was in almost all respects a more advanced industrial nation than England, when labor for wages in industrial establishments employing more than a dozen workpeople was even rarer in England than in France. As Professor McIlwain has told us, the medieval king or prince, for all his power, was not a despot. Despotism is not a medieval but a modern ideal of government. [6] Unlike the constitutional monarch of more recent times, the medieval king or prince had no superior in civil government, but his actual authority did not extend beyond distinct limits defined by tradition and custom. The lack of a generally-admitted right to tax the nation's wealth imposed one of the limits. The duties owed by the prince to God and to the Church imposed another limit, and a limit of some importance in an age when most men still believed in the Christian God. The local authority of feudal nobles, great churchmen, ecclesiastical foundations, municipalities, and even little mining communities imposed other limits.

In the sixteenth century, in both France and England, the crown was trying to extend its powers, and to supersede or at least to control all local authority. The crown was attempting, in Professor McIlwain's words, to replace "medieval constitutionalism with a new modern absolut-

[5] Cf. Nef, "In Defense of Democracy," *The General Magazine and Historical Chronicle,* vol. xlii (1939), pp. 17–38.

[6] C. H. McIlwain, "The Historian's Part in a Changing World," in *American Historical Review,* vol. xlii (1937), pp. 219, 223.

ism''. Was the English or the French king in the better position to carry on this struggle for absolute authority?

At the end of the fifteenth century the Spanish ambassador to England informed Ferdinand and Isabella that Henry VII ''would like to govern England in the French fashion but he cannot''.[7] As this remark suggests, the authority of the crown was greater in France than in England. But the difference was hardly great enough to explain entirely the success of royal absolutism in one country and its failure in the other during the next hundred and fifty years. It may be true, as an English historian has recently written, that at the accession of Francis I in 1515, ''absolutism was already so far established [in France] as to have become inevitable, [though] the view was not . . . clear to political thinkers of the day, who concurred in the opinion that France was a sort of limited monarchy''.[8] It is hardly true, except in the sense that everything which happens in the world must happen, that at the accession of Henry VIII, in 1509, government by a representative assembly was already so far established in England as to have become inevitable. The study of constitutional history during the last sixty years has made it difficult to maintain the position of Stubbs and Freeman that representative government was inherent in ancient English traditions. The recent rise in Germany of the most despotic government in western history has not helped to revive the old view of Stubbs and Freeman, prevalent in the nineteenth century, that the Germanic tribes who settled in England in the early Middle Ages brought with them the seeds of liberty, less freely scattered on French soil. While the house of commons had more influence on legislation than the states general, while it met more regularly and had a more definitely accepted place in the national government, the English crown at the accession of Henry VII had a large right to initiate bills and to veto those initiated by the commons. The share of the commons

[7] *Calendar of State Papers, Spanish,* vol. i, 1485–1509 (G. A. Bergenroth, ed.), 1862, p. 178.

[8] John S. C. Bridge, *A History of France,* vol. v, Oxford, 1936, p. 131.

in legislation was not great.[9] The Spanish ambassador who spoke of Henry VII's desire to govern after the French fashion was referring to the king's relations, not with parliament, but with his council, whose members he himself chose. He had already succeeded, the Spanish ambassador added, in getting "rid of some part of this subjection". "His crown is . . . undisputed, and his government is strong in all respects".[10] It would have seemed hardly less than revolutionary "to promote a bill for the restriction of the king's rights, the curtailment of his prerogative, or the control of his will".[11] Englishmen were still little more disposed than Frenchmen to question the power of their king to govern as he pleased, within the sphere where his right to govern was recognized. For a time it appeared that the Tudors might be almost as successful as the Valois in their efforts to enforce their personal authority and to extend it to cover a wider sphere.

In both countries the keys to absolutism were to be found partly in an extension of the sphere in which the king's right to govern was recognized, in an extension of the powers of the crown as over against the powers of local authorities of every kind, and partly in the setting up of a hierarchy of crown officials who would faithfully carry out the royal will. In legislative, administrative, and judicial matters the success of any policy of the crown in England depended more on the consent of private local interests than in France. As long as the English king wanted to do things that did not arouse the actual hostility of important sections of his wealthy, property-owning subjects, he was almost sure to have his way. Mr. Kenneth Pickthorn, today a member of parliament for Cambridge University, has described the situation very well in dealing with the kind of support which the first Tudor king, Henry VII, could reasonably expect from his justices of the peace. "What the class from

[9] Kenneth Pickthorn, *Early Tudor Government, Henry VII,* Cambridge, 1934, pp. 127–8.

[10] *Calendar of State Papers, Spanish,* vol. i, 1485–1509, p. 178.

[11] Pickthorn, *op. cit.,* p. 131; *passim;* and his *Henry VIII, passim.* Cf. Stubbs, *Constitutional History of England,* 5th ed., 1903, vol. iii, pp. 538–9.

which justices of the peace were drawn wanted done, Henry VII could get done very easily; what they did not mind being done, easily enough; what would happen if the crown should want done something which that class was determined should not be done, was a question still to be settled, even still to be raised".[12] The same thing might be said of the classes which dominated the house of commons, the boards of aldermen in the towns, and the common law courts. The members of these bodies were willing and even anxious to follow the king's will in so far as it did not differ from theirs on matters which they felt to be essential to their interests. The failure of royal absolutism in England is partly explained by the fact that the machinery of government, inherited from the Middle Ages and developed during the sixteenth and early seventeenth centuries, did not permit the English king as easily as the French king to act counter to the wishes of his chief subjects. It is explained perhaps to an even greater degree by the fact that, after the reigns of the first two Tudors and especially after the French religious wars, the matters on which the crown disagreed with its chief subjects were becoming more numerous and more important in England than in France. These matters were mainly religious, political, and economic. Much has been written about the personal influence of the monarchs and their ministers, and about the influence of religious and political issues, upon constitutional history. In this essay we are concerned with the economic and particularly the industrial issues.

For carrying out its policies the English crown depended mainly upon the good will of two social classes. The first was made up of the owners of substantial landed property in the country, the knights and gentlemen who held manors and the larger freeholders. The second was made up of the wealthiest merchants in the towns, the persons whose economic power was enabling them, especially after the Reformation, to form local political oligarchies and monopolize municipal authority to the exclusion of the craftsmen, trans-

12 Pickthorn, *Henry VII*, p. 72.

port workers, and small traders who formed the great majority of the municipal population. These two classes, the gentry and the merchants, provided the principal officers who governed for the crown throughout the land. During the hundred years which ended with the civil war the two classes tended to fuse. Their economic interests tended to become identical. The merchants were acquiring manors much more rapidly than in the Middle Ages. Their sons frequently deserted town interests for newly-acquired country interests; their sons' names appeared in the register of the privy council as local justices of the peace. Their daughters and widows frequently married the impecunious sons of lords or landed gentlemen who remained on their estates. The younger sons of the gentry and even of the nobility were going to the towns to seek their fortunes in trade and money lending, and those of them who were successful joined the governing class in the municipalities. The class from which most of the justices were recruited became the natural leaders in the country; the rich merchants became the natural leaders in the towns.

In France the church and even the old nobility played a somewhat greater part in government than in England. But in France after the religious wars, as well as in England, it was mainly from the landed gentry and the leading traders in the towns that the crown recruited the officials to enforce its will. During the hundred years from 1540 to 1640 certain important differences appeared between these classes in the two countries. While the gentry were tending to merge with the traders in both, the process was much slower in France. The crown was able to divest its servants of both classes from their local, private interests by two devices not used in England. First, by the creation of a new and lesser nobility, the *noblesse de robe,* made up of crown servants who purchased their offices and became partly and sometimes entirely dependent on the king for their livelihood. Second, by the appointment of officials to govern in provinces other than those of their birth, other than those where they had gained their fortunes from husbandry, industry, or commerce.

In France the royal administration was placed increasingly in the hands of persons whose main task was to serve the king, and who generally received an adequate salary for their services, after they had purchased their positions from other officials or from the crown. In England the royal administration was to a large extent in the hands of the justices of the peace, who were unpaid. They combined their private business with the king's service, and they often subordinated the king's interests to their own, by giving sparingly of their time to their official duties, and also, especially after the last decade of the sixteenth century, by giving a lukewarm response to orders from the privy council if these orders interfered with their business projects. If the justices themselves could not be counted on to give efficient and disinterested service to the government, this was even truer of their subordinates and assistants, who always had a great deal more work to do than they could possibly do well.[13]

The development of industry brought great changes in the interests of the gentry and the mercantile class in England. In the fourteenth and most of the fifteenth centuries industrial pursuits had been concentrated in the towns. In the late sixteenth and early seventeenth centuries the progress in mining and metallurgy, alum and salt making drew industrial labor into the country districts. The growth of new branches of the textile industry in Norfolk, Suffolk, and Lancashire, and of new branches of the metallurgical finishing trades in the neighborhood of Birmingham, produced a similar decentralization, because the merchants and their agents found it advantageous to put out wool, yarn, bar iron, and other raw materials to be worked on by village craftsmen who were not subject to the municipal and gild regulations of the old towns. At the same time the progress of mining, metallurgy, brewing, sugar refining, soap, alum, glass, and salt making greatly increased the capital

[13] Cf. E. F. Heckscher, *Mercantilism* (Eng. trans.), London, 1935, vol. i, pp. 246–50.

required to set up industrial plants both in the country and in the towns. Between 1540 and 1640, in an age when the annual wages earned by an unskilled workman seldom rose above £5 or £6 and almost never reached £10, the amount of capital invested in English industries in blocks so large as to exceed the means of groups of craftsmen or even substantial yeomen, ran into many millions of pounds. This capital was supplied mainly by the great town merchants and the gentry, by the same classes from which the crown recruited the officials to enforce its will. Thus the chief economic interest of some members of these classes was coming to be in the progress of industrial enterprise of a type which had been unimportant in the medieval economy.

In France, where large-scale enterprise made much slower headway, the chief economic interests of almost all members of the mercantile class and the gentry continued to be in local provincial trade, in the raising of grain, in the cultivation of grapes and olives, and in the leasing out of little mills or shops in and near the towns for the carrying on of industry on a small scale. The merchants and the landed classes were much less interested than in England in the progress of mines and small factories, and in the growth of the putting-out system on a large scale outside the towns.

In both countries at the time of the Reformation the relation of the crown to industry remained to be defined. A royal despotism could hardly be set up unless the crown exercised an extensive control over the economic life of the country. The success of royal despotism depended, among other things, on the extension of the power of the crown to collect revenue, and one of the most obvious sources of new revenue was industry. The protection of the public interest was also of concern to the French and English monarchs. If the power of medieval local authorities, feudal, ecclesiastical, and municipal, was to be supplanted by national government, it might be necessary for the crown to provide the consumer and the craftsman with the protection which in the past they had received from these local authorities. If markets became national, as they did in England, it might be necessary for national control to supplant local regulation. The protection of the poor from exploitation at the hands of the rich, the protection of the consumer from exploitation at the hands of the trader or craftsman, who were likely to charge high prices, give short measure, or sell wares of inferior quality, were widely felt needs. Many subjects, especially poor townsmen and peasants, believed it to be the duty of the crown to provide them with such protection. A school of thought was also growing up which held that if national industry was to develop, it must be protected by the crown from foreign competition and encouraged at home by crown subsidies. If the power of the crown to regulate industry and economic life in the public interest was not admitted, its power to exercise authority in matters of religion or foreign policy, even in matters of marriage with rival princely families, was likely to be weakened. While some of the motives for economic regulation conflicted with others, greater national regulation and control seemed imperative to every European monarch.

There were two principal ways of extending the control of the crown over industry. One was by the enactment and enforcement of codes and other laws designed to regulate conditions of industrial work. Such codes were generally best suited to the kind of industrial work which had predominated in the Middle Ages, that done in the homes of craft laborers or at little mills near by. The other was by the participation of the state in industrial enterprise, by the development of mines and manufactures on royal initiative or under royal protection.

CHAPTER 2

ROYAL INDUSTRIAL REGULATION [1]

Industrial Legislation in France.

During the hundred years following the Reformation, especially after the close of the religious wars at the end of the sixteenth century, the French kings re-enacted old laws and orders and passed new ones, greatly enlarging their sphere of industrial regulation. Thousands of royal acts (ordinances, edicts, letters patent, decrees, and *règlements*) dealing with industry were passed.[2] The mere task of formulating, copying, and distributing these acts, some of them printed but most of them written by scribes, must have occupied scores of officials in Paris and the chief provincial towns.

A large portion of all the enactments dealt with the organization in the towns of groups of craftsmen following the same occupation. One of the chief objectives of the

[1] The general subject of industrial regulation in France and England before 1789 has been discussed by Professor E. F. Heckscher in his recent book (*Mercantilism* [Eng. trans.], 2 vols., London, 1935). His treatment of that subject is, I think, fundamentally sound. I have made no attempt to go over the ground that he has covered rather thoroughly. My object in this section of my essay is different from the one Professor Heckscher set himself. It is to consider the relationship of government regulation in France and England to the great differences between the progress of industry in the two countries during the hundred years from 1540 to 1640. My obligations to Professor Henri Hauser's studies of French industrial organization are even greater than my obligations to Professor Heckscher, as will be apparent from the footnotes which follow. I regret that I have been unable to make use of Professor C. W. Cole's, *Colbert and a Century of French Mercantilism*, 2 vols., New York, 1939. It appeared after this essay had been written.

[2] In addition to the printed laws, I have studied the acts in Noël Valois, *Inventaire des Arrêts du Conseil d'Etat* (*règne de Henri IV*), 2 vols., Paris, 1886–93, together with the actual decrees in the Archives Nationales, série E, and in the Bibliothèque Nationale, MSS. Français and MSS. Clairambault; Archives Nationales, MS. Index to *Ordonnances* in the series X1A; *Ordonnances* and letters patent in the departmental archives in Toulouse and Marseilles.

crown was to strengthen the craft gilds and increase their number. The Middle Ages were not, as historians once supposed, the golden age of the gild *régime* in France. At the beginning of the sixteenth century most industrial work, even in the towns, was done by craftsmen who were not members of formal gilds.[3] The differences between a craft with a gild and a free craft were not always very marked, for the work done in both was regulated. When there was a formal gild, a group chosen from among the master craftsmen did the regulating; when there was no formal gild, the town government did it. Access to the mastership in a craft controlled by a gild was generally open only to apprentices who had worked for a prescribed period, who submitted satisfactory evidence of their technical skill, paid an entrance fee, and took the gild oath. Access to the mastership in a free craft was open on easier terms to a larger number of persons, including sometimes strangers from other provinces and even from foreign countries.[4]

Between 1540 and 1640 there was an increase in the proportion of all town craftsmen subject to extensive regulation and particularly to regulation by royal officials. As early as the winter of 1560–61 the states general, assembled at Orléans, made recommendations to the crown concerning industrial legislation. In response to one of their requests, a royal ordinance was prepared in 1561 permitting all gilds to revise their statutes and ordinances under the supervision of the crown, and, when authorized by the king, to have them printed. The main object was to prevent craftsmen from neglecting or breaking the rules of their gilds.[5] After the worst phases of the religious wars had ended in the reign of Henri IV (1589–1610), the movement to strengthen and extend the gild *régime,* begun before the

[3] Cf. Henri Hauser, *Ouvriers du temps passé,* 5th ed., Paris, 1927, pp. viii–x; Hauser, "Le travail dans l'ancienne France," in *Les débuts du capitalisme,* Paris, 1927, pp. 88–9, 103.

[4] Cf. Hauser, *Les débuts du capitalisme,* pp. 84, 110.

[5] Hauser, *Ouvriers du temps passé,* pp. 254–6, 259.

wars, made headway.[6]   Two famous edicts of 1581 and 1597 laid down uniform rules for the organization of handicrafts everywhere in France,[7] and aimed to organize all craftsmen in gilds.   While neither of these edicts was successfully enforced, formal gilds multiplied in most towns during the seventeenth century.   The second of the two edicts, which proved more effective than the first, enabled groups of master craftsmen not members of formal gilds to obtain from the royal officials the advantages enjoyed by the gilds. These advantages were now legally open to all craftsmen, because the edicts had made membership in gilds compulsory.   With the support of the crown, free crafts were adopting more and more restrictive forms of regulation, making it so difficult to enter them that many of the distinctions between free crafts and gilds disappeared.[8]   As royal officials gained increasing power over the municipal governments, they replaced the municipal officers, or dictated to them, when it came to regulating the free crafts.   At the same time the gilds found it desirable to have their own regulations confirmed by royal letters patent, as was proposed in the ordinance of 1561.[9]   As a result largely of the intervention of the crown in municipal industry, the gilds flourished during the reign of Louis XIV as they had never flourished in the Middle Ages.[10]   Industrial work in the towns was subject to more regulation than ever before.

[6] Hauser, *Les débuts du capitalisme*, pp. 94–5.   There were some setbacks. In Burgundy between 1615 and 1618 most of the large towns succeeded in getting Louis XIII to pass edicts, letters patent, and decrees abolishing the gild *régime*.   But the freedom thus acquired was incomplete and short-lived. Before the middle of the seventeenth century, the crafts in most of these towns were no less subject to gild regulations than they had been before 1615 (Hauser, ''L'organisation du travail . . . en Bourgogne,'' in *Les débuts du capitalisme*, pp. 126–60).

[7] Hauser, *Travailleurs et marchands dans l'ancienne France*, Paris, 1920, pp. 194–6.

[8] Cf. Hauser, *Les débuts du capitalisme*, pp. 110–13, 115.

[9] See on this Hauser, ''Les pouvoirs publics et l'organisation du travail dans l'ancienne France,'' in *Travailleurs et marchands*, esp. pp. 179 sqq.

[10] Cf. Hauser, *Ouvriers du temps passé*, p. x; *Travailleurs et marchands*, pp. 179–83.

The French kings and their ministers, together with the royal officials in the provinces, showed great skill in utilizing the gild and the municipal authorities as instruments for developing a national system of industrial regulation. This system was extended in some cases beyond the towns to workers in adjoining villages and bourgs.[11] Encroachments by the monarchy on gild activity went back to at least the middle of the fourteenth century, and they were numerous during the reigns of Louis XI, from 1461 to 1483, and Francis I, from 1519 to 1547. But the movement for royal control over the crafts became much more active after the passage of the edicts of 1581 and 1597.[12] These general laws, and the numerous decrees with which the council of state followed them up and sought to give them force,[13] were not the most important means by which the crown established rules for manual work. The general laws were re-enforced by many specific acts, regulating in much detail the conditions of work for a single gild in a particular town, or defining the precise work of each gild when a dispute arose between several competing groups of craftsmen. The rules enacted in 1615, in the form of an ordinance of thirty-three articles for the pewter makers of Paris, are typical of hundreds of such royal enactments. These rules of the pewter makers fixed the term of apprenticeship and the conditions for admission to the mastership. To prove their skill, all candidates, except the sons of masters, had to submit a piece of work (like our candidates for the doctor's degree). All pewter makers were forbidden to work Sundays and holidays, or before five in the morning and after eight at night. The materials which they might use in fashioning their wares, and the methods they must follow, were specified. They were prohibited from working anywhere except in their own homes.[14]

In drafting such regulations, the crown officials consulted the master craftsmen and frequently the town alder-

[11] Cf. Hauser, *Les débuts du capitalisme,* pp. 97–9, and see below, p.

[12] Cf. Heckscher, *op. cit.,* vol. i, pp. 138–9, 141, 144–6.

[13] Valois, *op. cit., passim.*

[14] Archives Nationales, X1A8647, ff. 478–81.

men. The gild often prepared its own rules,[15] which were always in accordance with the ancient practice of the craft and were generally based on earlier regulations. This procedure helped the royal officials to obtain the aid of the governors of each gild and of the municipal authorities in enforcing the royal enactments.

At the beginning of the sixteenth century the industrial workman in the towns was generally a craftsman who labored in his own home or at some little water-driven mill near by, with the help of his family and of one or two journeymen and apprentices. In some crafts, such as printing, where the presses and the type were too expensive for a manual workman to buy, access to the mastership was confined to employers of means, who sometimes performed little or no manual labor in their shops. Many workpeople, especially in the principal towns, could no longer expect to become master craftsmen. They had to work as journeymen for wages all their lives. Groups of these wage-workers had begun to organize themselves as journeymen, to keep up their wages and to insist on what they regarded as decent working conditions. The gild statutes and ordinances, granted or confirmed by the crown during the sixteenth and early seventeenth centuries, were rarely if ever of help to these journeymen in their efforts to improve their lot. The crown generally supported and extended the regulations of gilds or of groups of free masters fixing maximum wage-rates for journeymen. The policy was to maintain stable rates, not to lower rates. But during the sixteenth century, when the prices of food, wine, and fuel doubled or tripled and in some cases even quadrupled and quintupled, such a policy struck at the standard of living among the workmen. Manufactured products fashioned in the towns rose in price much more slowly than food, wine,

[15] E.g. Archives départementales de l'Aube (Troyes), C1948 (letters patent of 1621 concerning the master dyers of Troyes); Archives départementales des Bouches-du-Rhône, B3341, ff. 339, 363 (articles proposed by the pewterers of Lyons in 1584 for the regulation of their craft, and later, in 1602, applied also to the pewterers of Marseilles).

and fuel, which came from the country.[16]   The kings' advisers regarded the fixing of maximum wage-rates as a part of the royal policy of fixing the price of cloth and other commodities which town craftsmen produced.   Royal officials generally seem to have turned a deaf ear to the complaints of the journeymen over this wage-fixing policy, and to have threatened them with fines, whippings, imprisonment, and in some cases even with death, if they took higher wages than were legal.   While the regulations were sometimes evaded by mutual agreements between the masters and their journeymen, the policy of the crown had an influence in reducing real wages.[17]   Other regulations sanctioned by the royal officials or prepared by them, helped to prevent the journeymen in certain trades from becoming masters, and from participating in the government of the gilds.   Industrial regulations sanctioned by the crown were almost always more favorable to the employers than the wage-workers in those town crafts where a cleavage had taken place between capital and labor.[18]

In supporting the masters the king's officers were trying to maintain public order,[19] and to insist on the respect that servants were expected to show their masters, in an age when the principle of obedience to authority was still regarded as of fundamental importance by most Frenchmen.   Although the crown generally favored the masters in disputes with their journeymen, it was no part of royal policy to bring about a cleavage between employers and wage-workers in established crafts, to encourage the development of large industrial enterprises.   The proportion of all industrial workpeople who labored in considerable establishments in the towns was certainly small at the beginning of the sixteenth century.   The master who employed more than a dozen workers in his shop or mill was the very great exception.   The master who employed even

16 J. U. Nef, ''Prices and Industrial Capitalism in France and England,'' in *Economic History Review*, vol. vii (1937), p. 177.

17 Cf. Hauser, *Ouvriers du temps passé*, pp. 100–9, esp. p. 108.

18 Cf. *ibid.*, pp. 246–9.

19 Cf. *ibid.*, p. 233.

half a dozen workers was probably the great exception. Wage-work under the putting-out system was more common in the large towns than wage-work in the employer's shop. In the textile industry many a merchant paid wages to dozens of workpeople who labored in their own cellars or garrets on materials they had fetched home from his warehouse. Unlike the journeymen printers, such workpeople were not subject to supervision. They owned or rented their tools and equipment. They went for the yarn or the cloth they needed, now to the house of one merchant, now to that of another. Access to the mastership in their craft was not shut to them as frequently as it was to journeymen printers. If a census of all industrial workers in French towns had been taken early in the sixteenth century, it would probably have shown that the large majority were masters and apprentices, that only a small minority were wage-workers, and only an exceedingly small minority wage-workers who had no prospect of becoming masters.

During the sixteenth and early seventeenth centuries most of the royal regulations dealing with the town crafts were not of a kind likely to encourage the multiplication of enterprises employing more than a handful of wage-workers under one roof. It was not even of a kind likely to facilitate the employment of increasingly large numbers of wage-workers under the putting-out system. In almost every case outsiders were forbidden from entering a craft without having served an apprenticeship,[20] and the length of the term of apprenticeship was fixed, generally at three or four years. The number of apprentices a master could keep at a time was invariably limited, generally to one, or to two if one apprentice had already served for three years. Further rules were designed to interfere with industrial concentration. Thus the potters in one town were ordered in

[20] Exceptions were sometimes made for the sons of masters, and, on a few occasions (for example in the case of a cutter of marble, who was a foreigner and who set up a workshop in Paris in 1605), the crown by decree permitted individuals to follow an occupation without having been admitted to the craft (Archives Nationales, E5B, fol. 249, i).

1572 to reduce the number of wheels in their shops.[21] In 1610 a long series of enactments and legal proceedings, running as far back as 1480, were cited by the council of state in settling a dispute between the dyers of silk fabrics and the makers of gold, silver, and silk cloth at Tours, to prove that the crafts must remain separate, that no dyer ought to employ cloth makers and that no cloth maker ought to practice dyeing.[22] In Amiens, at the request of the aldermen and the gild of serge cloth makers, the council of state decreed in 1610 that all dealers in woollen yarn must sell it in the public market of the town, and only to masters of the craft.[23] The object was to prevent private merchants, not themselves manufacturers of serge cloth, from accumulating large stocks of yarn which they might get worked up on their own terms. Such rules hindered the growth of large enterprises, in which a single merchant or partnership of merchants could put out materials from a central warehouse to be worked up at piecework wages by many workpeople.

With the help of the town government, over which the crown exercised increasing control,[24] royal officials attempted to fix the prices of products and to regulate the methods of manufacturing. An edict of 1571 fixed the price of every kind of cloth throughout the realm. It prescribed the length and width of all pieces of woollen cloth in each province. It ordered that within four months all looms must be adjusted so that only cloth of legal size would be produced. Any looms not adjusted in time were to be broken by the royal officials and replaced by lawful looms. All cloth was to be marked with a leaden seal indicating the place of manufacture, and merchants were to be fined for buying or attempting to sell unmarked cloth.[25] An

[21] *Inventaire sommaire des Archives départementales, La Manche,* p. 81.

[22] Archives Nationales, E25B, fols. 226–7. For similar regulations by the *Cour de Parlement* at Troyes in 1631, see Archives départementales de l'Aube, E1140.

[23] Archives Nationales, E6A, fol. 185, i.

[24] Cf. Hauser, *Travailleurs et marchands,* pp. 179 sqq.

[25] Archives départementales des Bouches-du-Rhône, B3332, fol. 550.

edict of 1626 established a new set of royal officials in all the *bailliages* and *sénéchaussées* throughout the realm, to maintain the quality of iron wares and to prevent the use of unsuitable iron by certain metal workers, such as cutlers and the makers of locks and keys. The new officers were to visit all the iron forges in their jurisdictions at least once every month and see that all good quality iron was marked D for *doux*, and all inferior iron A for *aigre*. All traders and workers in metal were forbidden to buy unmarked iron. All bars of iron had to be made of a size specified in the ordinance.[26]

The crown often went still further and prescribed the exact ingredients to be used in dyeing [27] and in the manufacture of commodities like soap and beer. In all places where beer was brewed, officers were appointed by an edict of 1625 for the purpose of enforcing rules on the brewers in order to prevent the production of bad beer, which was said to cause colds, pleurisy, fevers, and other illnesses.[28]

The Enforcement of Industrial Legislation in France.

This elaborate system of industrial legislation, if enforced, was bound to make all change in manufacturing methods difficult. It was bound to interfere with the movement of labor from the home into any sort of small factory. How far was it successfully carried out?

The attempts of royal officials to enforce it often caused friction. In the printing industry at Lyons and Paris, the masters were in an almost continual state of war with their journeymen over wage-rates from 1539 until 1573.[29] Strikes were the ordinary weapon employed by the journeymen in their efforts to improve their lot. There were also occa-

[26] *Recueil général des anciennes lois françaises*, Paris, 1829, vol. xvi, p. 183–91. Edicts were passed authorizing the appointment of officials for inspecting leather and paper manufactured throughout the kingdom (Archives Nationales, E1C, fol. 56; Archives départementales de l'Aube, C2231).

[27] Archives départementales de la Haute-Garonne, B273, fol. 293.

[28] *Recueil général des anciennes lois françaises*, vol. xiv, pp. 154–8.

[29] Hauser, *Ouvriers du temps passé*, esp. ch. x.

sional riots by wage-workers in certain branches of the textile industry.[30]

These demonstrations against wage regulations were mainly the result of special conditions produced by the revolutionary increase in prices between about 1515 and about 1595. Bread, wine, and meat rose in price threefold and more in Paris and in some other towns. Riots took place only in the few branches of industry where a cleavage between masters and wage earners had caused a sharp divergence of interests. They were not directed against that part of royal industrial legislation designed to prevent industrial concentration.

When it came to other aspects of the regulations than those connected with wages or hours of labor, it was the master craftsmen who did most of the protesting. In a few trades like printing, where five or more workpeople were generally employed under one roof, the masters tried to prevent the enforcement of compulsory apprenticeship, and to get work done mainly by wage hands.[31] The complaints of such masters suggest that the enforcement of apprenticeship regulations was far more widespread in France than in England, for there, as we shall see, objections seem to have been raised more frequently by wage-workers, who wanted the laws enforced, than by employers who objected to their enforcement.

Acts of apprenticeship were entered with increasing regularity during the sixteenth and early seventeenth centuries in the books of the local notaries,[32] who kept records of almost all business transactions. Like most public officials in France, these notaries had no private interest in business. As readers of that charming play of Alfred de Musset, *Le Chandelier,* will remember, the notary has occupied a position in French life only less important than the priest. In the late sixteenth and seventeenth centuries, as

[30] Professor Hauser cites very few examples of such outbreaks, and I have not found any examples to add to his.

[31] Hauser, *Ouvriers du temps passé,* pp. 205–7.

[32] I have examined scores of notarial contracts of apprenticeship in the Archives départementales du Var. Cf. Hauser, *Ouvriers du temps passé,* p. 23.

in more recent times, he visited the poor sick man who wanted to make his will, as well as the rich town merchant who wanted to draw up an agreement for leasing a house, a mill, or a farm in the suburbs. To enter into a contract without the assistance of a notary seemed as strange to most Frenchmen as to die without the consolation of the sacrament. Every detail of the contract was written into the notary's book, so that it could be examined at any time. Tens of thousands of these books have come down to us, and a large proportion of them are now stored in various French archives. Filled out in the sixteenth and early seventeenth centuries in a hand intelligible to contemporaries, though often too mysterious for any but the paleographer to decipher today, these books gave a formality and even a sanctity to all agreements that they never had when they were a matter of private arrangements between individuals without such elaborate intervention by a public official. The notarial system helped to make the evasion of the apprenticeship regulations more difficult than in England, where no systematic and detailed records of apprenticeship contracts were kept.

While attempts to evade the apprenticeship obligation may have grown increasingly common in the late sixteenth and early seventeenth centuries, when the gild system was extended to new industries and new places, a study of documents connected with several industries in the south of France suggests that there, at least, most craftsmen served the regular apprenticeship required by law.[33] Even in a comparatively new industry like paper making, which had come to employ many hands since the invention of printing in the fifteenth century, we find that the masters generally went through an apprenticeship in Provence and Languedoc, even in country villages where there were no formal paper-making gilds. The master provided his apprentice with food and often with clothing. He was bound to look after him when he was sick, and in general to take the place of his parents during the time of his apprenticeship.

[33] Cf. the *Inventaires* of the departmental archives for Gard and Var.

The enforcement of apprenticeship regulations gave the French royal officials less trouble than the enforcement of the regulations providing for the inspection of various wares to make sure they conformed to government specifications. In 1590 the king's council was informed that a revolt had broken out among the leather makers in Lyons, Troyes, Rouen, Le Mans, and Caen against the enforcement of an edict of 1586, appointing officers to inspect and mark leather and leather goods. The craftsmen were reported to have tried to massacre some of the special officers appointed to enforce the edict, and the crown called on the local magistrates to punish the guilty.[34]

There was little disposition on the part of the crown to relax the regulations in the face of opposition, as was frequently necessary in England. The opposition came not, as in England, from the enforcing officials. It came from the master craftsmen. In the dispute among the leather workers of various towns, royal officials were instructed to carry out all the clauses of the edict to which objection was taken, "notwithstanding any opposition or appeals".[35] In spite of opposition by the *parlement* of Normandy to an order of 1603 by the king's council, appointing a certain Pierre Mazire to inspect all metal in Rouen and other towns, Mazire was ordered to carry out his commission.[36] There is no evidence that the officials were often lukewarm, as they generally were in England, about enforcing the enactments.

The authority of the king over the French crafts increased during the late sixteenth and early seventeenth centuries. It was used to preserve the forms of industrial organization which had prevailed on the eve of the Reformation, and to discourage the development of large private enterprises. Before the time of Colbert (1661–1683), with whom the establishment of extensive royal regulations over industry is sometimes associated, the crown already possessed almost as much authority as a royal despot could desire.

[34] Archives Nationales, E1C, fol. 58.
[35] *Ibid.*
[36] *Ibid.*, E18A, fol. 60.

Industrial Legislation in England.

In England, as in France, the crown was attempting by national regulations to confine manufactures to groups of trained and apprenticed workmen, to fix prices and wages in the public interest, to interfere with the concentration of workmen in a single enterprise, and to protect the consumer by insisting that industrial products should be of good quality.

During the Middle Ages the proportion of the entire population living in towns was probably somewhat smaller in England than in France. But as there was apparently no important English town where nearly all the crafts were free, as they were at Lyons, it is possible that a larger proportion of town craftsmen were members of formal gilds in English than in French towns. In England, as in France, the gilds had been used by the king as executive agents to help in the regulation of economic life.[37] It might seem, therefore, that the crown was in as good a position in England as in France to control craft industry with the help of the gilds. But during the late sixteenth and the early seventeenth centuries the gild system was beginning to break down in England, at the very time when it was being strengthened and extended in France. New industries were developing much more rapidly than in France, in the old towns, in the country, and in places like Manchester and Birmingham, which had been villages but were growing into centers for manufacturing.

The crown attempted to meet the changing conditions by incorporating many new companies, like the tobacco pipe makers, the gun makers, and the spectacle makers in London and other towns where these crafts were practiced. Many older gilds, which had changed their nature, were incorporated by the crown as livery companies. These companies were seldom associations of manual workers. The woodmongers gild of London, whose members had handled the carriage of wood and charcoal to the city before the reign of Elizabeth, was turned into a company of rich whole-

[37] Heckscher, *op. cit.*, vol. i, p. 225.

sale traders in coal. Its members were mostly wealthy London merchants who had started their careers as dealers in other commodities—haberdashers, grocers, and ironmongers—and who found new openings for profit as London grew rapidly, and became dependent for its fuel on the arrival of great fleets of colliers from Newcastle.[38] The gild, especially in London, was proving an elastic form which skillful traders could easily stretch into something resembling an employers' association or ring, for keeping up the prices of commodities and eliminating competition from independent merchants.

Unlike the French kings, the English monarchs were not able to make extensive use of the gilds to help in enforcing industrial regulations. No laws were passed, like the French edicts of 1581 and 1597, making membership in gilds compulsory. The efforts under James I and Charles I to extend the control of town gilds over industry to the suburbs and to country villages were generally unsuccessful, like the more ambitious attempts to create companies to control the cloth and the beer manufacture of whole counties.[39] During the seventeenth century, when the regulation of craftsmen by gilds and municipal governments was increasing in France, free craftsmanship was becoming the general rule in England. The corporate towns multiplied. But the gild system was not extended to the new towns, and some of the old towns apparently lost their gilds. In 1689, when there were two hundred towns in the kingdom, only one in four had any organized gild.[40] In spite of the efforts of the king's councillors during the reigns of James I and Charles I, the privy council was unable to find in the government of the gilds an agency capable of giving the crown effective aid in its attempt to control the industrial life of the nation.

[38] Cf. J. U. Nef, *The Rise of the British Coal Industry*, London, 1932, vol. i, pp. 406–8.

[39] Heckscher, *op. cit.*, I, pp. 233–5, 238–44. Cf. pp. 284–5. On beer see below, p. 30.

[40] Heckscher, *op. cit.*, I, p. 243.

For industrial legislation the crown had to depend mainly upon the enactment of statutes by parliament, upon royal proclamations and letters patent, and upon orders of the privy council or decrees issued by the same body sitting in star chamber. For the administration of these enactments the crown had to depend mainly upon justices of the peace and their subordinates, and in the towns upon the other municipal officials. The gilds played only a small and diminishing part in the administration of the industrial laws.

In England there was no lack of general laws applicable to all industries, or at least to all the workers and masters in a single industry throughout the realm. But England had fewer special acts than France to help enforce the general laws, or to provide industrial codes for particular sets of craftsmen.

The most celebrated and important of all the English enactments was the lengthy statute of artificers of 1563. When reprinted, it sets up to some twelve pages of small type. Contemporaries called it that "industrious longe lawe".[41] Among other things, the act was designed to maintain, extend, and facilitate the enforcement of, the medieval rules insisting that craftsmen should serve a term of apprenticeship, and to regulate the wages paid by masters and by merchants who put out materials to be worked up by laborers in the towns and country villages. All workmen were obliged to serve as apprentices for seven years, so that there was no variation in the length of apprenticeship to suit the different kinds of training required for the various crafts, such as was obtained in France by the system of special royal enactments. The statute also fixed the hours of labor and aimed to prevent a workman from leaving his master without a testimonial.

The statute of artificers was only the most comprehensive of many acts regulating industrial conditions, passed by parliament between the death of Henry VIII, in 1547,

[41] Cf. M. R. Gay, "Aspects of Elizabethan Apprenticeship," in E. F. Gay, *Facts and Factors in Economic History*, Cambridge, Mass., 1932, p. 134.

and the outbreak of the civil war. A national policy, of medieval origin, which aimed to fix the prices of grain, bread, and ale, was maintained and extended to include the prices of beer and of the malt used in brewing.[42] For a time an attempt was also made to fix, by order of the privy council, the prices of building materials, especially bricks,[43] and also the wholesale prices of coals in London.[44] A set of statutes, based on medieval legislation, aimed to prevent the movement of industry away from the old towns into the country, but all this legislation was relaxed by the parliament of 1575–76, and completely swept away by that of 1623–24.[45] Two series of statutes dealt with cloth making and leather making. They laid down elaborate rules concerning the methods which should be employed in manufacturing. The cloth-making statutes fixed the length, breadth, and weight of various kinds of cloth and the size of warping bars. They authorized royal officials to mark cloths with discs or seals to help the purchaser to know their quality, and to search the warehouses of textile traders and craftsmen for defective goods. They prohibited the use of certain newly-discovered machines, known as ''gig-mills'', in dressing cloth, on the ground that the wire cards, with which these machines were equipped, damaged the fabrics.[46] Fullers and cloth finishers were forbidden to employ weavers under their roofs and thus increase the size of their enterprises. Similar rules were prescribed for most other industries. An attempt was made to fix the size of bricks.[47] Statutes were passed regulating the quality of the malt and

[42] See, e.g., *Acts of the Privy Council*, 1596–7, pp. 542–4; *Calendar of State Papers Domestic*, 1581–90, p. 706; 1625–6, p. 522; 1629–31, p. 396; *North Riding Quarter Sessions* (Atkinson), vol. ii (1612–20), *passim;* cf. Heckscher, *op. cit.*, I, p. 225.

[43] State Papers Domestic, James I, vol. cxii, no. 80; *Calendar of State Papers Domestic*, 1639, p. 64.

[44] Nef, *Rise of the Coal Industry*, II, pp. 280 sqq.

[45] Heckscher, *op. cit.*, I, pp. 238–9.

[46] Heckscher, *op. cit.*, I, pp. 263–4. Cf. State Papers Domestic, Charles I, vol. ccxxxxiv, no. 1; Stella Kramer, *The English Craft Gilds*, New York, 1927, p. 163.

[47] *Calendar of State Papers Domestic*, 1619–23, p. 460.

the hops used in brewing,[48] with the object of reducing disease and drunkenness, especially among the poor. The privy council issued orders which aimed to insure the good quality of the materials used in the manufacture of soap and glass.[49]

In 1593 a courtier named Robert Zinzan asked Burleigh, who was then the lord treasurer, to grant him a patent to "survey" the sugar refined in and near London and prevent the use of eggs, clay, and lime in its manufacture. Zinzan's proposal was rejected, probably because of the strong reasons urged against it by Richard Carmarden, a customs official who had established himself with Burleigh as one of the most loyal and disinterested of the queen's servants. Carmarden showed that the process Zinzan asked to reform was an indispensable part of sugar refining, and that the proposed survey might drive the manufacture to Hamburg and Holland.[50] Zinzan's proposal was apparently rejected on the ground that it would not improve the quality of the sugar. The claim of the crown to survey industrial products in the interest of the consumer survived. In the reign of James I, plans were on foot to prevent the sale of bad coal, lead, beer, and tobacco, by granting royal patents of surveyorship like the one Zinzan had sought.[51] At least one surveyor's office was set up.[52]

The authority of the crown was being used to fix the number of producers, as well as to fix the prices of their products and to prescribe their methods of production. Restrictions on the number of enterprises were imposed in industries such as printing, brewing, iron-ore smelting, sugar

[48] 2 and 3 Edw. VI, c. 10; 1 James I, c. 18.

[49] E.g. State Papers Domestic, Charles I, vol. ccclxxviii, no. 58; vol. ccclxix, no. 95.

[50] State Papers Domestic, Elizabeth, vol. ccxlv, nos. 48, 48 (i), 52; Nef, "Richard Carmarden's 'A Caveat for the Quene,'" in *Journal of Political Economy*, XLI (1933), pp. 34–5, 37–41. Cf. *Calendar of State Papers Domestic*, 1595–7, p. 98.

[51] Nef, *Rise of the Coal Industry*, II, pp. 240 sqq.; State Papers Domestic, James I, vol. cix, no. 164; *Calendar of State Papers Domestic*, 1611–18, p. 606; 1619–23, p. 138.

[52] See below, pp. 53–4.

refining, brick and tile making,[53] where no attempt was made to set up monopolies in the hands of royal patentees, as well as in industries such as the manufacture of alum, glass, and gunpowder, where for a time such monopolies were established.[54] The most rigid restrictions were those imposed on the printers in 1586. At that time there were in London twenty-five printing houses with fifty-three presses. A decree of the star chamber forbade any increase in their number, and allowed only two other printing establishments in all the rest of the kingdom, one in Oxford and one in Cambridge.[55] By the reign of Charles I, the principle of a fixed maximum had been abandoned. The privy council left it to the discretion of the archbishop of Canterbury and the bishop of London to limit the number of printing houses. In 1635 half the master printers in London had not been licensed.[56] A new decree of the star chamber in 1637 aimed to restrict the practice of printing to licensed masters.[57]

Brewing in the corporate towns was restricted to persons licensed by the municipal authorities. An attempt was made as early as 1620 to extend these restrictions to the whole realm.[58] Under Charles I a certain Captain James Duppa, the author of a scheme for arming the coal ships against pirates and foreign men-of-war, became the moving spirit behind the plan to confine the brewing industry everywhere to licensed brewers.[59] He and a man named Sir Abraham Williams were appointed royal commissioners for malting and brewing. In 1637 Duppa was trying to organize all the licensed brewers of Kent into a corporation, and to get the king to incorporate them by letters patent.[60]

[53] For sugar refining and brick and tile making, see State Papers Domestic, James I, vol. lxxxvii, no. 74; lxxxviii, no. 98; cxxxi, no. 36; Charles I, vol. ccclxxii, no. 58 (i).

[54] See below, pp. 88–98, 107–11.

[55] State Papers Domestic, Elizabeth, vol. cxc, no. 48; Nef, ''A Comparison of Industrial Growth in France and England,'' p. 657.

[56] State Papers Domestic, Charles I, vol. ccvii, no. 85.

[57] *Ibid.*, vol. ccclxxvi, no. 15.

[58] State Papers Domestic, James I, vol. cxii, no. 75.

[59] Nef, *Rise of the Coal Industry*, ii, p. 265; Privy Council Register, vol. xlvi, p. 434.

[60] *Calendar of State Papers Domestic*, 1637, p. 579.

In the interest of timber conservation, statutes and proclamations were passed under Elizabeth and James I prohibiting the making of iron and glass in certain areas. As the shortage of timber increased in the reign of Charles I, the privy council tried to prevent the establishment of new furnaces and forges without the permission of the royal officials.[61]

During the eighty years preceding the civil war, Elizabeth and her two Stuart successors did everything in their power to build up a comprehensive system of industrial regulations to cover the expanding manufactures of the country. Their objectives resembled very closely those of the French kings who were their contemporaries. They sought also to regulate wages in the national interest. The wage regulations were somewhat more favorable than in France to the workpeople who wanted to maintain or improve their material standard of living.

In France the old medieval practice of fixing a maximum wage for an indefinite period was continued throughout the sixteenth century, in spite of the extraordinary rise in prices. But in England the statute of artificers of 1563 called upon the justices of the peace to "rate and appoint wages" in their districts afresh each year. This added to their already heavy load of duties. Fixing wages was a complicated matter calling for much technical knowledge, especially in the textile industry where most craftsmen, who worked in their homes on materials received from clothiers and merchants, were paid by the piece. The new law obliged the local justices to reconsider every twelve months a whole series of wage rates applicable to spinners and weavers for yarn of various qualities and for cloth of various sizes.[62] While one object of frequent wage assessments was to prevent wages from rising above what seemed a reasonable level, the adoption of the principle of yearly assessments made it possible to adjust the legal rate to meet the rise in the cost of living and to avoid flagrant injustices,

[61] E.g. State Papers Domestic, Charles I, vol. cvii, no. 25; vol. cccxxi, no. 42; vol. ccccxiii, no. 119.

[62] See e.g. State Papers Domestic, Elizabeth, vol. ccxliv, no. 130.

which were bound to occur with rising prices when the rates were fixed for a much longer period. A statute of 1603 established a policy still more favorable to wage earners, particularly to spinners and weavers in the woollen cloth-making industry. The yearly rates fixed by the justices of the peace were to be a minimum, and the clothiers who put out their wool, yarn, and cloth to be worked on by the local craftsmen, were to be fined not, as in the past, for paying more than the legal rate, but for paying less. The privy council was behind this new policy of fixing a minimum wage, and during the years from 1629 to 1640, when Charles I tried to govern without parliament, it brought greater pressure than ever before to bear on the local justices to keep up wages.[63] The wage policy of the king and his council was less likely to satisfy clothiers and other industrial employers in England than in France. This English policy of adjusting wages to maintain the workers' standard of living, caused friction between the king and many of the subjects upon whom he had to depend for support in parliament, and for the administration of statutes, proclamations, and privy council orders in the towns and villages.

In England, as in France, the new industrial legislation of the late sixteenth and early seventeenth centuries placed many obstacles in the way of wealthy men who wanted to establish private enterprises for manufacturing on a larger scale than had been common in the past. But these obstacles were less formidable than in France, because the English regulations, except in printing, were somewhat less rigid and uncompromising than the French regulations. To begin with, many important districts in England were exempted from the application of particular industrial laws. Those counties where rural enterprise was common were not subject to the acts designed to restrict industrial enterprise to the towns. Again, the number of apprentices and journeymen a master might employ was less strictly limited

[63] R. H. Tawney, ''The Assessment of Wages in England by the Justices of the Peace,'' *Vierteljahrschrift für Sozial- und Wirtschaftsgeschichte*, XI (1913), pp. 311, 313–14, 316, 321, 326, 332, 534–5, 542–52.

than in France. There were fewer rules against the use of new machinery and against the concentration of a large number of tools and machines in a single plant. The statute of artificers allowed persons apprenticed to a craft to exercise it anywhere, and not, as in France, only in the place where they had been trained. This permitted English workmen a greater liberty of movement than French workmen.[64] It permitted a larger degree of private initiative among employers. The greater mobility of labor made it much less necessary than in France for rich merchants and landlords to ask the crown for special privileges when they wanted to assemble workpeople in large numbers to labor in some new industrial enterprise, such as a soap-, a glass-, or a paper-making factory.[65] The English regulations limiting the number of masters who could practice a craft did not always work against industrial concentration, as they did in the printing industry, where a limit was imposed on the number of presses as well as on the number of houses. In brewing, the attempts to confine the manufacture to licensed brewers, in so far as they were successful, encouraged concentration.[66] These regulations hindered alehouse keepers, innkeepers, and victuallers, as well as common householders, from making beer in a small way in their shops and homes. Thus the regulations encouraged the brewers, who were generally in a larger way of business,[67] to increase their output.

The industrial laws enacted between 1558 and 1642 were somewhat less comprehensive in England than in France. They were somewhat less hostile to the concentration of capital and labor under private management. They occasionally had the support not only of wage earners and master craftsmen, but of wealthy merchants who had invested in manufacturing enterprises. These merchants generally

[64] Cf. Heckscher, *op. cit.*, I, pp. 266, 239, 231, 230.

[65] Cf. below, p. 58.

[66] See e.g. State Papers Domestic, James I, vol. cxii, no. 75; Charles I, vol. cccxlviii, no. 34; Privy Council Register, vol. xlvi, p. 434; *Calendar of State Papers Domestic*, 1619–23, p. 490; 1637, pp. 49, 579.

[67] See e.g. *Hist. MSS. Com.*, 14th Report, Appendix, Part viii, p. 142.

had interests in manufactures, and some of the new laws served their purposes by interfering with competitors who tried to start rival enterprises.[68]   But the regulations which the privy council wanted to enforce were almost never liberal enough to satisfy a large number of those wealthy merchants who were exploiting the opportunities for industrial development provided by the very rapid growth of mining and manufacturing after about 1575.   When these merchants wanted to invest in country industries, when they wanted to make use of new machinery and modern technical methods, when they wanted to employ large numbers of unapprenticed wage-workers, when they wanted to compete with established manufacturers or to buy the products of a monopoly artificially maintained, they were always confronted with statutes, proclamations, decrees, or letters patent which seemed to entrench on their liberties as individuals.   None of the new regulations satisfied all the powerful merchants.   The restrictions against starting new sugar refineries imposed during James I's reign, for example, had the support of various rich haberdashers, merchant tailors, ironmongers, and grocers of London, who owned the established refineries.   But the majority of the grocers, who had no share in the profits from the manufacture, were opposed to the restrictions, because they increased the price of the sugar they had to buy.[69]   By James I's reign, and even before, the powerful town merchants and improving country landlords who were inconvenienced by the industrial regulations had begun to outnumber those who benefited by them.

English industry was hedged in at every turn by what would seem to a nineteenth-century liberal, as it was beginning to seem to a progressive merchant in the reigns of James I and Charles I, a highly complicated and very comprehensive system of industrial regulations.   If Englishmen differed as to the desirability of these regulations, they believed almost unanimously, though not altogether cor-

68 See below, p. 55.
69 State Papers Domestic, James I, vol. lxxxvii, no. 74 (ii), (iv), (v).

rectly, that England had a system of laws for the government of industry no less complete than that of France. That impression endured in the eighteenth century. One English writer in 1766 put it that "the difference between us and France consists chiefly in this: . . . we are [as] remarkable [as they] for good laws, but are shamefully neglectful in their execution".[70] By his time the English government had given up any serious attempt to enforce the laws. This had not been the trouble in the late sixteenth and early seventeenth centuries. At that time the privy council kept a great number of officials busy about the administration of the laws. The courts were full of cases brought by the attorney-general against private capitalists and local authorities who had broken them. What were the results of these efforts at enforcement?

The Enforcement of Industrial Legislation in England.

When Queen Elizabeth came to the throne in 1558, the administrative machinery at her disposal for enforcing the industrial laws was less satisfactory than that of the French king. Like her two Stuart successors, she had in the privy council, with its offshoots, the council of the north and the council of Wales and the Marches, a group of powerful public officials, most of them chosen by the monarch, and hardly less devoted to the interests of the monarchy than the French king's council (*conseil du roi*), with its three principal sections, the *conseil d'état,* the *conseil des finances,* and the *conseil des parties.* But it was not possible to govern the scattered industries of the country by decrees and orders from above alone. For carrying out any industrial policy, the central administration had to depend upon the local authorities, municipal or provincial, which it could utilize or create. For the enforcement of any industrial policy, the central administration had also to depend upon the courts to punish persons who broke the laws. So the queen and her ministers were largely dependent for the suc-

[70] M. Postlethwayt, *The Universal Dictionary of Trade and Commerce,* 3rd ed., London, 1766, vol. i, p. iii.

cessful execution of their policies upon the mayor and aldermen in the corporate towns, upon the unpaid and overburdened justices of the peace there and elsewhere, upon the judges in the common law courts, and to a lesser extent upon the judges in special courts such as the courts of chancery of the palatinates of Lancaster and Durham. In France the local authorities who enforced the royal enactments and the judges who tried offenders had more time for their duties than in England, and they were more in agreement with the policies they were asked to administer.

During the eighty-five years which followed the accession of Elizabeth and culminated in the civil war, the privy council was not able to strengthen the royal authority for enforcing industrial legislation by introducing new, disinterested officials into the local administration to help the justices of the peace in performing the increasingly heavy duties imposed on them by the new enactments. But in France the royal administration in the provinces was made much more effective and more disinterested, especially after the accession of Henri IV in 1589, when the worst phases of the religious wars came to an end. Before the death of his successor, Louis XIII, in 1643, the attempt to apply the gild *régime* to all craftsmen in the towns had met with partial success, and the king's ministers had found in the government of the gilds an important agency to help them in the local application of industrial laws. The control of the king's officers over the municipal government had increased in a large number of towns, so that the king's ministers were able to count on the support of the municipal authorities to a much greater extent than in England. They had, in addition, a hierarchy of royal officers in every province, including those officials specially appointed to enforce particular industrial regulations such as the inspection of iron and of leather. The generally recognized need for reorganizing the provincial administration after decades of civil war gave Henri IV an opportunity to send out to various provinces special commissioners, with full power to establish order and carry through a program of administrative reform. Soon the king gave some of these commissioners permanent posts, and they became the first *intendants des provinces.* They were tried servants of the crown. Though often recruited from the merchant class, they renounced their private business interests before they assumed the duty of enforcing the royal will. Richelieu strengthened their powers during Louis XIII's reign. Before the king's death, in 1643, the *intendants* had begun to build up a new and more efficient local administration in the provinces, side by side with the administration of older royal officials, the *baillis* and *sénéchaux* and the *gouverneurs,* who frequently had more private local interests than the *intendants.* The *intendants* gradually took over the functions of these officials until their offices became largely honorary. The king's ministers were able to rely on the new officials to enforce the royal will with greater loyalty and efficiency than any of their predecessors.

Between 1589 and 1643 the royal officials in Paris and the provinces found it possible to bring an increasing proportion of all disputes over industrial legislation into the royal courts,[71] where the judges were likely to uphold both the letter and the spirit of the royal acts. This was done partly by appeals from local courts, but even more by invoking the principle of *cas royaux,* by claiming that the issue was one of concern to the king and that it could be properly tried only in a royal court. Since the edicts of 1581 and 1597 established royal authority over the gilds, all disputes concerning gilds could be made *cas royaux.* Disputes involving matters of public interest, and particularly matters of public order, were subject to trial in the royal courts, and there were few industrial disputes which could not be brought under one head or the other. In France the king's interest and the public interest were fused in the mind of most subjects, especially after the civil wars of the late sixteenth century had convinced them that unity under the king was the best, and perhaps the only, means of securing domestic peace. As Malherbe wrote in his cele-

[71] Cf. Hauser, *Travailleurs et marchands,* pp. 183–4.

brated ode to Henri IV's new queen, Maria de'Medici, upon her arrival at Aix in 1600, the future of the nation was felt to depend on the strength of the royal family.

> Ce sera vous qui de nos villes
> Ferez la beauté refleurir,
> Vous, qui de nos haines civiles
> Ferez la racine mourir.

In England attempts similar to those made in France, to extend the jurisdiction of the royal courts, the court of star chamber, the court of requests, and the court of high commission, were met by an effective opposition from the common-law courts. Common-law judges claimed that their decisions could overrule those given in the royal courts. They even went so far as to maintain that common law was superior to statute law. So jealous of their rights were the common-law judges, and so influential were they in the house of commons, that the whole system of royal jurisdiction, which the Tudors had carefully cultivated, was swept away by act of parliament in 1641, on the eve of the civil war. In the early seventeenth century the power of the king and his advisers to enforce their will in matters of industrial regulation was undermined in England at the very time when it was greatly strengthened in France.

All we know about the history of apprenticeship regulation suggests that the monarchs were much less successful in England than in France in their attempts to enforce the laws. This is explained in no small degree by the rapid expansion of old industries and the introduction of many new ones. The apprenticeship provisions of the statute of artificers, like the provisions of the French edicts of 1581 and 1597, were intended to apply to workpeople in all occupations, in the villages as well as the towns. But the rules for apprenticeship were legally applicable only to workers in industries carried on in 1563, when the statute was passed.[72] New industries multiplied in England during the next eighty years. The population was growing, and the

[72] Cf. State Papers Domestic, James I, vol. lxxxvii, no. 74 (iv and v).

workpeople employed in the expanding industries were recruited by the masters from the poor and the unemployed, sometimes from distant counties. They were brought to their new work without any technical preparation for it. Even in those industries, like mining or smelting, which were practiced long before 1563, it was not feasible to enforce the apprenticeship regulations when the size of the plant increased rapidly. During the late sixteenth and early seventeenth centuries a great many enterprises were started, employing scores of wage-workers in a single plant —in the mining of coal and some ores, in iron, copper, brass, and wire making, in alum, soap, salt, and glass manufacturing. There is nothing in the apprenticeship clause of the statute of artificers to indicate that workers in these industries were exempt, though in an earlier clause a number of such occupations were placed in a different category from the thirty "sciences, craftes, mysterys or arts" in which no one was allowed to work for less than a year. The baser industrial pursuits enumerated were "the diggynge seeking, fyndinge, gettinge, meltinge, fynynge, workinge, trying, makinge of any Sylver, Tynne, lede, Iron, Coper, Stone, sea coole, stone coole, moore Coole or Cherk cole, [and] beinge occupied in or aboute the makinge of any glasse".[73] Whatever the intention of the authors of the act may have been, there is no evidence that the privy council or the justices of the peace ever tried to apply the apprenticeship regulations to such occupations as these. Almost every year hundreds and sometimes thousands of workmen were recruited to serve in them and in the new industries. There was, in consequence, a continual increase in the proportion of industrial laborers to whom the apprenticeship regulations were inapplicable.

In other industries, especially in the various branches of textile manufacturing, we find the justices of the peace frequently asked to enforce the rules of apprenticeship, and to prevent fullers and cloth finishers from employing weav-

[73] 5 Eliz. c. 4, para. ii, v. As printed in R. H. Tawney and E. Power, *Tudor Economic Documents*, London, 1924, vol. i, pp. 340–1.

ers under their roofs. There were many prosecutions for failures to carry out the regulations of the statute of 1563, in the courts of quarter sessions, held by the justices of the peace, in the county assizes, and in the great common law courts at Westminster.[74] In spite of these prosecutions, the proportion of unapprenticed workpeople in the textile industry was already very large in the reign of James I.

By that time Norwich, the chief center of the rapidly growing cloth manufacture of East Anglia, had become the most populous town in England after London. A large part of its inhabitants gained their living by textile work. In 1610 the efforts made to enforce the apprenticeship regulations in the town seemed so half-hearted to the workmen lawfully trained in worsted weaving, that a group of apprentices and journeymen, numbering about a hundred, decided to strike against the abuse. They seized on the only kind of organization for craftsmen known to them, and sought to form a gild of strikers with four wardens. According to the account that has come down to us in the state papers, they agreed "that neither Mr. Mayor nor their Maist-ers should 'bring them to their worke againe untill such tyme [as] there were some order taken that such that hath not bin prentyce to the trade . . . aswell strangers as Englishe were suppressed. . . ."

The mayor got wind of this plan before the day appointed for the strike. He complained to the privy council of a conspiracy and combination tending to tumult and sedition. The ringleaders in the movement were brought to trial before the lord chief justice, though their only offense had been a threat to take action which would have helped enforce the apprenticeship provisions of the statute of artificers, which the mayor himself, as a public official, should have upheld.[75]

In spite of subsequent attempts by the privy council to enforce the law, there is no evidence that the proportion of

[74] Cf. M. R. Gay, ''Aspects of Elizabethan Apprenticeship,'' in E. F. Gay, *Facts and Factors in Economic History*, 1932, pp. 134–63.

[75] State Papers Domestic, James I, vol. liv, nos. 62, 62 (i), 62 (iii).

unapprenticed workpeople in Norwich, or in East Anglia generally, was reduced after 1610. Some years later, in 1617 or 1618, the worsted weavers of Norwich and Norfolk, together with other textile workers of Essex and Suffolk, complained to the privy council that the employment of unapprenticed weavers in all their crafts was a great abuse, and that fullers of cloth kept looms in their houses contrary to law. The council ordered that the statutes against both practices be enforced, that all the industrial laws be applied to worsted weaving and every branch of textile work introduced since the statute of artificers.[76] These orders proved ineffective. In 1622 the justices of the peace in Suffolk reported that many thousands of workers in the county, two-thirds of all those employed in the textile industry, had not served an apprenticeship. They told the council it was useless to try to suppress these unapprenticed workpeople, though they promised not to allow new laborers to enter the textile industry unless they had served an apprenticeship.[77] In the light of the previous history of the apprenticeship regulations in East Anglia, it is not likely that they made good their promise.

The attempted strike at Norwich suggests that the local magistrates, in whose hands the administration of the industrial regulations had been placed, were often more interested in punishing lawful apprentices, who made a disturbance over their failure to enforce the law, than in enforcing it. Some of the decisions of common-law judges help us to understand why the magistrates could afford to neglect their duty in this matter of enforcement. By the reign of James I, there were many judges who felt no enthusiasm about enforcing the letter of the apprenticeship regulations. Some of them were eager to exploit every kind of legal technicality to reduce the number of crafts subject to the regulations.[78] They insisted that the statute of artificers was subject to the common law, and that com-

[76] *Ibid.*, vol. civ, no. 97.
[77] *Ibid.*, vol. cxxix, no. 59.
[78] Cf. Heckscher, *op. cit.*, I, p. 291.

mon law did not forbid men from working at a craft without special training.[79] A case tried in 1615 in the court of king's bench, over which Sir Edward Coke presided as chief justice, shows the lengths to which some judges went in defending the right of workpeople to labor without serving an apprenticeship. The case is a well-known one. It concerned a man named Tolley. He was a Londoner who had taken up the work of an upholsterer after serving his apprenticeship as a wool packer. As was pointed out in the judgment, Tolley was within his rights because the so-called "custom of London" permitted craftsmen who had been apprenticed to any trade in the city to practice any other.[80] In the opinion of the court, this custom "hath had a perpetual allowance", and could not be altered in any way by the statute of artificers. That was enough to acquit Tolley, but it was not enough to satisfy the judges. The judgment proceeds to give several reasons why Tolley would have been innocent if he had become an upholsterer without serving any apprenticeship. Upholstery was not subject to the apprenticeship clause because it was not "a trade . . . mentioned in any one of the branches of the statute". Later, as if the court feared lest this interpretation of the act should make the apprenticeship clause applicable to all the sixty-one "trades and mysteries" actually mentioned, the judgment stated that upholstery was not subject to the statute, "for it is not mentioned within that branch that concerneth the compelling of men to be Apprentices". As no industries were mentioned within that branch, such a ruling might have made the clause inapplicable to any industry! Apparently the intention was to limit its application to "such [trades] as required Art or Skill for the managing of them". The judgment proceeded to define trades requiring skill. ". . . An Husbandman, Tankard-bearer, Brickmaker, Potter, Miller, and such like Trades, are not within the Statute of 5 Elizabeth cap. 4, . . . for they are arts which require rather ability of body than skill: But a

[79] Stella Kramer, *The English Craft Gilds*, New York, 1927, p. 161.
[80] Cf. Heckscher, *op. cit.*, I, p. 245.

Brewer and Baker are within the Statute, because it concerneth the health of mens bodies to have good Bread baked and beer brewed. . . ." [81]

This judgment was not a model of logical reasoning. It was more difficult to interpret such an interpretation of the statute than to interpret the statute itself. If taken literally, the words of the court made it possible at the very least to exclude most manual occupations, at a time of great development in those industries requiring mainly bodily exertion instead of fine craftsmanship. The proportion of all industrial workers employed in highly skilled trades—"sciences craftes mysterys or arts" as they were called in the statute of 1563 [82]—was diminishing every decade. In England the judges were obviously interpreting the laws to conform with the new industrial practices. In France there were fewer new industrial practices with which to make the laws conform.

There is no way of estimating for the early seventeenth century the proportion of all master craftsmen and industrial wage earners who had not served an apprenticeship for seven years in the occupation they were following, as the act of 1563 required. If we could determine the proportion in the textile industry we should go some way toward determining the proportion in all industries, because the textile industry, with its endless ramifications, probably employed at least a third of the industrial workpeople in the country. The proportion of unapprenticed workers in the textile industry in East Anglia, one of the three chief centers of cloth making in England, was certainly large. In Lancashire, which formed with the West Riding of Yorkshire another of the chief centers, the proportion was larger in all probability, for Lancashire had fewer corporate towns than East Anglia, and the enforcement of industrial legislation was especially difficult where there was no municipal

[81] Tawney and Power, *Tudor Economic Documents,* I, 378–83; Heckscher, *op. cit.,* I, pp. 292–3. My attention was called to this case by Professor Heckscher's discussion of it.
[82] 5 Eliz. cap. 4, para. ii.

government and, in consequence, no medieval precedent for such regulation.[83]   In the southwest, the third of the chief centers for cloth making, the percentage of unapprenticed workpeople was probably as large as in Lancashire.[84] Spinners were never apprenticed and it was only in the finishing processes, dyeing, fulling, and dressing, that a seven-year apprenticeship was at all general.   The number of workers in the finishing trades was small compared to the number of spinners and weavers.

After textiles, the building industry probably employed the largest number of industrial workpeople during the early decades of the seventeenth century.   Like woollen cloth making, most branches of the building industry had an ancient history and had been established crafts long before the enactment of the statute of 1563.   That did not prevent widespread evasion of the apprenticeship requirements by builders and their workmen in London and the neighborhood, where hundreds of new houses were built almost every year during the reigns of James I and Charles I. A petition presented to the privy council about 1613, by the plasterer's company of London, illustrates some of the difficulties of getting the law enforced.   The plasterers were an old gild.   They had been granted a royal charter more than a hundred years before, and an act of the common council of the city had made it illegal for bricklayers and other builders to get their plastering done by workmen who were not members of the company.   When breaches of this act became frequent at the beginning of the seventeenth century, the privy council tried to stop them by appealing to the lord mayor and aldermen to enforce it.   That did not get at the root of the trouble, for as the population doubled and tripled, London was sprawling out farther beyond the city limits almost daily.   As the plasterers wrote, ''the abuses formerly complained of are farr more frequent in

[83] A. P. Wadsworth and J. de L. Mann, *The Cotton Trade and Industrial Lancashire*, Manchester, 1931, pp. 54–5, 59–61; Heckscher, *op. cit.*, I, pp. 238–41, 243–4.

[84] In the opinion of Mrs. Godfrey Davies, the former Miss M. R. Gay, who plans to make a study of the textile industry in this area.

Middlesex and Surrey then in the Citty, to the great wrong and Prejudice of the said Companie''. Bricklayers, tilers, and carpenters in those counties, who had contracted to build for persons of quality and others, ''for lucre and saveing to themselves, ymploie the poorest and weakest workemen that will doe the worke cheapest and exclude yor Peticoners to their great wronge and far greter to the subject''.[85] Good workmanship was giving way before cheap workmanship. Of what use was it for an old gild, like the plasterers, to enforce the apprenticeship requirements among its own members, if they were deprived of the means to practice their skill by the competition of unskilled laborers? The gilds were bound to become lax in maintaining their old standards. It is not surprising to find the privy council complaining, in 1637, that brick and tile makers, who were dependent for employment (like the plasterers) upon bricklayers and tilers, had among their number persons ''untrained and unskilfull in the trade''.[86]

Brick making was one of those crafts which the court in the Tolley case regarded as unskilled and therefore not subject to the act of 1563. In that case brewing was regarded as subject to the act. Yet the enforcement of the apprenticeship regulations was far from universal in brewing. Shortly before the civil war there were complaints in Nottingham that brewers had set up in the town without authorization from the municipal authorities.[87] In London, the great center both for building and for brewing, so many brewers had failed to comply with the apprenticeship regulations that there seemed little sense in trying to enforce them when, in 1638, the charter of the brewers' company came before the king for renewal. The attorney-general and the elder Sir Henry Vane, a leading representative of the gentry whose son-in-law was one of the principal Newcastle colliery owners, recommended that members of the

85 State Papers Domestic, James I, vol. lxxv, no. 77.
86 State Papers Domestic, Charles I, vol. ccclxii, no. 81.
87 *Ibid.*, vol. cccxlviii, no. 34 (i).

company be allowed to brew even though they had not served an apprenticeship.[88]

With the very great changes in industrial life taking place in England, especially between 1575 and 1620, an increasingly large number of leading merchants and improving landlords acquired interests in the new mines and manufacturing enterprises. Many of them were also magistrates. The apprenticeship regulations hampered them in employing unskilled laborers at low wages.[89] As time went on, the number of magistrates willing to enforce the regulations diminished. On the eve of the civil war, the industrial workpeople who had not served the apprenticeship required by law were probably more numerous than those who had, even in the textile industries and other trades where an attempt was still made to apply the regulations. If we include the workers in heavy industries like mining and metallurgy, unapprenticed workpeople almost certainly formed the great majority.

Meanwhile in France there was no such expansion of heavy industries as in England during the late sixteenth and early seventeenth centuries. There was no such wholesale evasion of apprenticeship requirements in old crafts. Work in the home remained more common than in England; the progress of industry beyond the old town limits was slower. Most of the large enterprises in France had been established with the help of royal privileges.[90] The craftsmen in them often received a training even more fastidious than that given by the masters in the ordinary craft gilds, for a great many of the royal manufactures were established for fashioning artistic wares, such as tapestries and crystal glass vessels, and the laborers employed had to be taught skill and taste. A regular apprenticeship remained part of the normal upbringing for any youth in France who planned to work with his hands, at a time when multitudes all over England went into industry without having served the apprenticeship prescribed by law.

[88] *Ibid.*, vol. cccc, no. 20.
[89] Cf. Kramer, *op. cit.*, p. 186.
[90] See below, pp. 58-9.

Were the other regulations embodied in Tudor and early Stuart industrial enactments any more effectively administered than the apprenticeship regulations? Where it was difficult to make craftsmen serve an apprenticeship, it was usually even more difficult to enforce other regulations.[91] The power of the gilds to supervise industry and trade in general was bound up with their power to enforce apprenticeship. When any considerable number of unapprenticed workers practiced a craft, the regulative authority of the gild in all directions was inevitably undermined, because the unapprenticed workpeople were outside its control. There was little possibility of maintaining old standards of workmanship or refusing to allow legally apprenticed members of the gild to use new machinery, when outsiders were producing similar goods more cheaply by new methods. The apprenticed workpeople had the choice of adopting the new methods or of going idle. The municipal authorities and the justices of the peace, upon whom the successful administration of royal enactments chiefly depended, were in a position similar to that of the governors of the gilds. Before they gave up their attempt to enforce the apprenticeship regulations, they generally abandoned their attempt to enforce other industrial regulations. Even as late as the eighteenth century, when the justices of the peace no longer went through any of the motions of enforcing the other provisions of the statute of artificers, they continued to try persons for breaches of the apprenticeship clause.[92]

In the sixteenth and early seventeenth centuries, the privy council was as eager to have the local authorities control prices and wages as to have them enforce the statutory apprenticeship requirement. Many members of the council were determined to protect the poor by keeping down the prices of grain, bread, ale, and beer, as well as to protect the spinners and weavers by fixing reasonable wage rates in the cloth-making industry. The strong line taken

[91] Cf. Kramer, *op. cit.*, pp. 162–3.

[92] I also owe this information to Mrs. Davies, who has in hand an essay on the enforcement of the apprenticeship regulations.

by Queen Elizabeth's privy council was maintained by the councils of her two successors, in spite of the growing difficulties of wage and price fixing, caused by the growth of new, large industrial enterprises and the continued rise in prices produced by the inflow of American silver. During the period from 1629 to 1640, when Charles I tried to govern without parliament, the privy council took, if anything, a firmer and more consistent position than ever before in favor of enforcing all industrial legislation.[93] In its administrative capacity, the council made more demands than its predecessors upon the justices of the peace and the sheriffs, to carry out the wage and price regulations. In its judicial capacity, sitting in the star chamber at Westminster, the council punished breaches of the regulations more severely than in the past. A clothier was kept in prison until he had paid three of his former workers more wages than he owed them. A corn dealer, who had hoarded a stock of grain, was heavily fined and forced to appear in the pillory at several prominent places in London, with a placard "for enhancing price of corn" tied to his hat, as the iron frame held his face forward staring at the crowds.[94]

Many justices of the peace took their obligations to keep down prices seriously, at least until after the accession of James I, in 1603. But as the civil war approached, and causes for opposition to the king's policies grew among the magistrates, their zeal on behalf of the royal service diminished. Although orders from the privy council kept them at a high pitch of activity in fixing prices and drafting wage assessments, their activity was of little advantage to the poor. Between 1590 and 1640 the prices of grain and bread seem to have risen almost everywhere more rapidly than the prices of any other commodities except lumber and firewood.[95] The municipal authorities in London held a special stock of coal to supply the humblest citizens with

---

[93] Tawney, *op. cit.*, p. 551; Heckscher, *op. cit.*, I, pp. 256, 258.

[94] Heckscher, *op. cit.*, pp. 258, 260.

[95] Nef, "Prices and Industrial Capitalism," in *Economic History Review*, vol. vii, no. 2 (1937), p. 166 and *passim*.

fires at a low cost. But they did not increase the stock between 1603 and 1640, in spite of the rapid growth in the population of London and the phenomenal rise in the cost of firewood. The price paid by the poor at the municipal yards rose much more rapidly than the price on the Tyne, whence the coals were shipped, and more rapidly than the price at several places in the south of England.[96]

The privy council had rather better luck in keeping up wages than in keeping down prices. Between 1590 and 1640 wage rates apparently rose about as rapidly as the cost of living.[97] The changes in the methods of assessing wage rates, introduced by the statute of artificers of 1563 and by another statute of 1603, contributed to this result. But under James I and Charles I the justices of the peace did little or nothing to help the council with its policy of raising wages.[98] The wages actually paid appear to have been more frequently above than below the legal rate. If the justices had cooperated wholeheartedly with the privy council, wage rates would probably have risen more than they did.[99]

Acts regulating methods of manufacturing, limiting the number of enterprises that might be established in an industry, and the number of apprentices a master might employ, were even less successfully administered than acts dealing with prices and wages. Early in the seventeenth century, if not before, masters often took many more ap-

[96] Nef, *Rise of the British Coal Industry*, II, p. 261. For coal prices in Cambridge, see *ibid.*, pp. 404–5 or J. E. Thorold Rogers, *History of Agriculture and Prices*, vol. v, pp. 398–404. For coal prices in the south of England as worked out by the International Scientific Committee on Price History, see Nef, ''Prices and Industrial Capitalism,'' p. 171. (The first volume of Sir William Beveridge's *Prices and Wages in England* (London, 1939) does not contain the table of coal-price relatives that he kindly placed at my disposal when I was preparing my article.)

[97] Nef, ''Prices and Industrial Capitalism,'' pp. 173–4; cf. pp. 164–5.

[98] Heckscher, *op. cit.*, I, pp. 260–1.

[99] Tawney, *op. cit.*, pp. 563–4; Heckscher, *op. cit.*, I, p. 261. A new work on the subject of wage regulation that I have not had time to consult is R. Keith Kelsall, *Wage Regulation under the Statute of Artificers*, London, 1938.

prentices than the law allowed.[100] Even the printers, who were under closer observation than other masters because almost all their shops were in the shadow of the court at Westminster, failed to adhere to the limits imposed on the number of apprentices. In 1635 nineteen master printers in the city employed between them forty illicit apprentices.[101] Breaches of the statutes regulating cloth making were so common even in Elizabeth's reign that a pamphleteer remarked in 1577, "better laws [for the trade] cannot be made, only there wants execution".[102] That complaint was to be heard again and again in the course of the next decades. In the early seventeenth century the justices of the peace continually showed their distaste for the laws regulating the technical side of cloth production.[103]

Even when the justices were willing to enforce these laws, they were always finding difficulties in their way. Thus in April, 1633, two justices in Gloucestershire attempted to enforce the cloth-making regulations in the local textile industry. They issued orders forbidding the use of mills for dressing cloth, as contrary to statute. The clothiers who dealt in cloth and provided the spinners, weavers, and fullers with the materials to work up in their homes, were asked to present themselves at the places where the cloths were finished and where the magistrates searched the fabrics for defects before affixing their seals.

Three months later the spinners, weavers, and fullers, who went to the warehouses of the clothiers for supplies of wool, yarn, and cloth, were out of work and threatened with starvation, because the clothiers had refused to carry on their business under the rules issued by the justices. When asked to explain their refusal, the clothiers wrote that the April orders threatened them with financial ruin. It was impracticable to enforce the statutory regulations as the local justices were trying to do. It would take two years to

100 Cf. Kramer, *op. cit.*, p. 186.
101 State Papers Domestic, Charles I, vol. cccvii, no. 88.
102 Quoted Heckscher, *op. cit.*, I, p. 251.
103 Heckscher, *op. cit.*, I, pp. 260–1.

find the materials necessary to dress cloth by hand instead of by mills. The clothiers could not afford to give the time to be present when the cloths were sealed, for some of them lived as far as ten miles away, a ride of two or three hours over muddy paths.[104] If the justices and the privy council wanted cloth making to continue, the April orders must be withdrawn.

The action of the clothiers placed the local magistrates in a dilemma. Unless they yielded and stopped enforcing the law, they might have to provide for thousands of unemployed.

Unemployment had become very common in the cloth-making industry in the seventeenth century. In the early twenties there had been a great depression in the cloth trade which had lasted several years. The increasing unemployment gave the merchants who put out materials an excellent opportunity to challenge the statutory regulations, which interfered with the use of new machinery and with other technical changes designed to reduce the costs of making cloth and to increase their profits.

In opposing the orders of April, 1633, the Gloucester-shire clothiers claimed that their "moseing mills" were legal because they were not the "gig-mills" prohibited by statute. The "moseing mills" were equipped with teazels, the "gig-mills" with wire cards, for dressing the cloth. All over England the merchants and industrial masters were resorting to technical quibbles of this kind to evade the statutory regulations.

Many of the industrial regulations which the privy council asked magistrates to enforce were not embodied in statutes. They were based simply on royal proclamations or letters patent, or on orders of the privy council. The authority of parliament was not behind them. In such cases, they could often be attacked without resort to any kind of

[104] State Papers Domestic, Charles I, vol. ccxliv, no. 1. Denials of the right of royal and of gild officials to search the houses of craftsmen and traders for defective goods became common in the seventeenth century (cf. Kramer, *op. cit.*, p. 163).

technical or legal quibble. While in France the authority of the crown to legislate, independently of the states general and even of the *parlements,* was strengthened at the beginning of the seventeenth century, in England the authority of the crown to legislate independently of parliament was weakened. No one appears to have questioned the legality of royal patents not specifically ratified by parliament until the last years of Elizabeth's reign. But after her death, in 1603, the Stuart kings found increasing opposition to their proclamations, letters patent, and council orders, partly because these acts frequently interfered with the profits of powerful merchants and landed gentlemen interested in the progress of large-scale industry. It became almost impossible for the privy council to enforce any industrial regulations, not embodied in statutes, if they conflicted with the private interests of such merchants and gentlemen. One of the chief difficulties in the way of enforcement is illustrated by two cases of different kinds. The first involved a royal monopoly of grinding grain in Bridgwater, the large port in southwestern England on the Bristol Channel. The second involved a royal inspection of coal shipped from Newcastle-on-Tyne.

In 1585 by letters patent Queen Elizabeth granted Bridgwater a new charter. A clause was inserted binding the mayor, recorder, and aldermen not to allow anyone to brew or sell any beer and ale in the town unless the malt and other grain had been ground at certain water-driven mills called Little Mills. These mills were owned partly by the crown and partly by the Earl of Hertford. Some twenty-five years later, in 1609 or 1610, a prominent citizen of the town named Robert Chute built a horse mill for grinding malt, for his "owne private gaine". Chute was mayor of the town and a justice of the peace, so his duty to uphold the brewing clause of the municipal charter was clear. Yet he not only permitted brewers and others to desert Little Mills for his horse mill, he brought pressure to bear on them to do so. He used the power of his office against some who did not. He had a part of the water supply diverted from

Little Mills, and this prevented the two wheels there from turning steadily during dry summers. He had his wife talk with persons who took their grain to Little Mills. Mrs. Chute went to see the son and the maid of a Mrs. Newman, who kept a fairly large stock of malt. According to the maid, the mayor's wife had said, "whie doe not your Dame grind her mault at my husbands horsemill. I hope you were well used [there]". Richard Newman, the son, testified that Mrs. Chute had been sharper and plainer with him. She had threatened that if his mother did not take her malt to the horse mill, "Mr. Maior would looke aboute". And, sure enough, he did. A week later Mrs. Newman was arrested and taken to prison. Her husband was fined 20s. at the next quarter sessions. When charges were brought in the court of exchequer against Chute for defying the brewing clause of the town charter, his witnesses defended him on the ground that Little Mills had not a sufficient supply of water to grind all the malt consumed in Bridgwater. As Chute had deprived Little Mills of part of its supply, this was not surprising! Chute's witnesses also testified that the brewing clause had been inserted not for the general welfare of the townspeople, but for the private advantage of John Courte, another prominent citizen, now dead, who had held from the queen a lease for three lives of her part in Little Mills when the town was granted its charter. Courte's son and widow were still getting a profit from this part when Chute built his horse mill.[105]

If the authority of the crown was not strong enough to maintain for a generation a monopoly of milling at Bridgwater, it proved too weak to support for even a few months royal patentees in their efforts to inspect the coal shipped from the Tyne valley, the chief source of fuel for the people of London by the end of James I's reign. Complaints from housekeepers and craftsmen about the quality of coal grew numerous and vociferous at the end of the sixteenth and beginning of the seventeenth centuries, when the shipments from the north were doubling or tripling every decade. It

105 Exchequer Depositions by Commission, 9 James I, Hilary 17.

was alleged that the colliery owners at Newcastle mixed good house coals, suitable for burning in the kitchen, the bedroom, and the parlor, with an inferior grade fit only for making lime or salt, and then sold the mixture at the same price as the best coals. The proposed remedy was to create at Newcastle an office of "surveyor of coals". The surveyor and his agents were then to examine every shipment, and issue a certificate, describing its quality, for the shipmaster to show the London wholesale dealers when he bargained with them for the sale of his cargo. The surveyor was to charge 4d. on each chaldron for his services, a tax that might have brought him upwards of £2000 a year toward the end of James I's reign. On at least three occasions between 1616 and 1637 the office of surveyor was created by proclamation and was granted by letters patent to royal favorites. But the surveyors were never able to make the colliery owners and shipmasters submit to the inspection, accept the certificates, or pay the tax. In the autumn of 1618, when the shippers who brought coal to London were penalized for refusing to recognize the surveyor's authority, they are said to have come in multitudes to the star chamber in Westminster seeking redress. No support for the patent of surveyorship was forthcoming from the chief municipal officers, the mayor of Newcastle and the lord mayor of London, for the mayor was usually a leading colliery owner and the lord mayor was influenced by the coal shippers who frequently held office in the city government. The most telling objection brought by the colliery owners and the shippers against the survey was that the proceeds from it would line the pockets of a private individual, whose interest was not the general welfare but his own gain. "How [may it] stand with the good of the common wealth," the colliery owners asked, "to raise so great a yearly sume out of so needfull a comoditie, and as it were out of the smoake of every mans chimney to the benefit onely of one private gentleman?" [106]

As the Bridgwater mill case and the quarrel over the coal

[106] Nef, *Rise of the British Coal Industry*, II, pp. 240–51.

surveyorship show, the enforcement in England of proclamations, patents, and orders of the privy council was increasingly bound up with private interests. There were fewer salaried servants upon whom the king could rely to help enforce the royal will than in France. There, in spite of the sale of royal offices and a great deal of corruption, the authority of the crown in economic matters retained an impersonal and respectable character which it was losing in England. In attempting to carry out any policy of industrial regulation, the privy council was faced with the alternative of appealing for support to the local magistrates or of entrusting the administration to royal favorites. The local magistrates often participated in the enterprises the council was seeking to regulate, and the royal favorites often solicited the office or the creation of the office for the emoluments it promised them. When the magistrates were zealous in enforcing the council's orders, it was generally discovered that the orders were helpful to the private interests they represented. The motives of members of the privy council itself were not above suspicion. In 1615 and 1616, for example, the council twice refused to allow a prominent denizen, who had assembled £6000 in capital, to build a new sugar refinery. It was reported that the archbishop of Canterbury was the chief stumbling block in the council. According to a report, he was "altogeather against" the project, "the raither for that his brother is one of them that are interested" in the existing refineries.[107]

Many English business men were coming to feel that the industrial acts limiting their liberty to seek profits were frequently sponsored and even inspired by other individuals who were seldom disinterested, and who were often self-seeking interlopers. Such a feeling helped them to break industrial laws with a freer conscience than Frenchmen.

A comparison of the history of government regulation in

[107] *Calendar of State Papers Domestic,* 1611–18, p. 396; State Papers Domestic, James I, vol. lxxxvii, no. 74; cf. nos. 74 (iv) and (v).

France and England shows that in both countries an attempt was made in the late sixteenth and early seventeenth centuries to have the crown regulate the whole industrial life of the nation. It shows that in France the enactments went farther than in England. Even if legislation had been effectively enforced in England, industrial enterprise would have been somewhat freer than in France, and there would have been less interference with the progress of large-scale industry. But the great difference between the two countries was not in the nature of the laws; it was in their enforcement. In France the officials were so vigorous about enforcing the laws that craftsmen sometimes tried to massacre them for their zeal. In England the officials were so lax that workmen sometimes struck in an effort to remind them of their duty. Breaches of the regulations grew so common in England, especially after the accession of James I in 1603, that government control was breaking down in spite of all the efforts of the king and the privy council to extend and even to maintain it. In France the situation was reversed. Government control was extended under both Henri IV and Louis XIII, from 1589 to 1643, and it became increasingly effective.

The difficulties in the way of enforcing industrial regulations in England were numerous, and they grew increasingly serious as the civil war approached. Enforcement of regulations governing the technical methods of manufacturing might dislocate the industry of a whole county, by throwing thousands of laborers out of work. The enforcing officials were generally lacking in enthusiasm for the regulations. When they were not, it was usually because they had themselves devised the regulations to restore their private fortunes. One difficulty led to another. So, as time went on and large-scale industry grew more important, all difficulties multiplied. The chief difficulty was that most of the regulations were of a kind that interfered with the progress of capitalist industrial enterprise, and that the financial interests of many officials came to be bound up with the development of mines, small factories, and large putting-out enterprises. As magistrates, the officials were placed in the position of having to enforce legislation which, as private persons, they found it desirable to evade. As time went on their personal interests were becoming stronger and their sense of responsibility to authority weaker. Some began to feel that their material interests as individuals might prove a better guide to conduct, a more promising means of promoting human welfare, than the ancient principle of obedience to civil government. This feeling found expression in the philosophies of Bacon and of Hobbes, though Bacon himself remained in politics a king's man and Hobbes, in his timidity, would not run risks to challenge the authority of either king or parliament. These philosophers, in their turn, began to influence the thought of their contemporaries. Their writings helped merchants, improving landlords, and magistrates to believe that material improvement might legitimately be made the chief objective of man. The new philosophy, as John Donne wrote, called "all in doubt", but it gave men a new staff to guide them on their path through life. That staff was natural science. As Bacon pointed out in his *Advancement of Learning,* first published in 1605, natural science "shall be operative to the endowment and benefit of man's life; for it will . . . minister and suggest for the present many ingenious practices in all trades. . . ".[108] The industrial laws often interfered with the application of these ingenious practices. Merchants and landlords, who were interested in their application, had little difficulty in concluding that the fault lay with the laws. The new philosophy fortified Englishmen in their disposition to forget their civil obligations and to remember their rights as individuals. It is no wonder that the chances of enforcing the industrial regulations of the king and the privy council diminished with every succeeding decade.[109]

[108] *The Works of Francis Bacon,* London, 1803, vol. i, p. 79.
[109] Cf. Conyers Read, "Mercantilism," in *The Constitution Reconsidered,* New York, 1938, esp. p. 70.

CHAPTER 3

ROYAL PARTICIPATION IN INDUSTRIAL ENTERPRISE

The industrial laws which have hitherto concerned us were applied mainly to manufactures that had flourished during the later Middle Ages in the towns.   Medieval conditions persisted in French to a much greater degree than in English industry during the late sixteenth and early seventeenth centuries.   But new and larger industrial enterprises were sometimes started even in France.   The policy of the French kings was to participate in the formation of nearly all of them by grants of special privileges and often of government subsidies in the form of land, buildings, and advances of cash.   By the reign of Louis XIV, in the second half of the seventeenth century, it had become difficult to start any considerable new enterprise without the permission and support of the royal administration.

At first sight there appears to be an important conflict between the objectives of the crown in this policy of industrial participation and in that of regulating industrial life through the gilds and the provincial and municipal officials. With one hand, the king was encouraging and even subsidizing large, heavily-capitalized ventures; with the other, he was enforcing enactments designed to interfere with industrial concentration.   But the French kings seldom subsidized large enterprises at the expense of small ones.   In established branches of industry, small independent shops and mills were absorbed into the system of royal manufactures without losing their identity.   It was chiefly in new branches of industry that the crown supported large enterprises.   By participating in them the king preempted a field that would have remained open to private investment.   The effect was to interfere with the natural concentration of capital in the heavy industries, by making the investors dependent for success upon royal favors more than upon economies in the costs of production.

The power of the crown to direct industry outside the gilds in France was based mainly on three attributes of sovereignty which the English parliament and the English courts denied in the seventeenth century. In the first place, the king claimed the right to administer all enterprises necessary for the defense of the realm. Secondly, he claimed the right to dispose of certain natural products, especially ores and minerals and salt, even when they were found in privately-owned lands. Thirdly, he claimed the right to endow certain persons with a temporary and sometimes a permanent monopoly of certain branches of manufacturing in particular towns or provinces. During the hundred years or so from 1540 to 1640 the French kings and their ministers managed to strengthen all these claims.

The Saltpetre and Gunpowder Manufactures in France.

Royal control over the saltpetre and gunpowder industries was based mainly on the importance of supplies for national defense. Gunpowder was probably introduced into Europe from China before the end of the thirteenth century. It did not revolutionize the conduct of war until the fifteenth and sixteenth centuries. At the time of the Reformation when the French king, Francis I, and the emperor, Charles V, embarked upon their military struggle for the domination of Europe, they found an adequate supply of firearms and gunpowder as indispensable for victory as an adequate supply of brave troops. Surgeons accompanying their armies had to improvise methods of dealing with hundreds of wounds from gunshot and cannon balls after every fierce engagement. Kings and princes throughout Europe saw the necessity of building arsenals at strategic towns in their dominions and stocking them with ordnance, gunpowder, and the saltpetre needed to make it. One after another the chief European rulers declared monopolies over the manufacture of saltpetre and gunpowder, shot and cannon balls, muskets and artillery pieces. Their advisers set about to devise the most efficient methods of providing these munitions in large quantities.[1]

In France the master of the royal artillery at Montpellier was given authority to requisition supplies of saltpetre throughout Languedoc for the king's service as early as the middle of the fifteenth century, when the hundred years war with England drew to its end. The manufacture of saltpetre without royal permission was declared illegal.[2] Before the death of Francis I a century later, in 1547, royal storehouses and magazines for ammunition had been built in many French towns. The main problem was to provide enough saltpetre earth. As this was obtained from the incrustations of old buildings and from the waste products of men and animals in outhouses, cattle sheds, pigeon- and dove-houses, it was necessary to enlist the services of saltpetre makers in many towns and some villages to gather the material in every province. The amount of saltpetre required for the king's service was determined by the royal officials every year or so. In 1547–8, for example, the annual quota for the kingdom was fixed at some 400 tons.[3] Quotas were then assigned to the various provinces, and production in the provinces was parcelled out among a large number of towns. This method of dividing responsibility between the various territorial divisions and subdivisions of the country was the same followed in collecting the most important of all French taxes, the *gabelle* and the *taille*.

[1] For the munitions monopolies set up in 1511 and 1515 by the Archduchess Margaret of Austria, as sovereign-governess, in Franche-Comté, and, as regent of the Netherlands, in Hainaut, see Archives départementales du Nord (Lille), B713, B1192. At the beginning of the seventeenth century, when the southern Netherlands came under the rule of the Spanish Archduke and Archduchess Albert and Isabella, they confided their monopoly of saltpetre and gunpowder making to a courtier named Jacques Le Roy (*ibid.*, B1836, ff. 60–63, 135 sqq. See also Archives départementales du Pas-de-Calais (Arras), B4, f. 202). In Lorraine the dukes maintained a similar monopoly as an attribute of sovereignty (Archives Nationales, K875, no. 18).

[2] Archives départementales de l'Hérault, A3 (Commission pour ramasser . . . le salpêtre . . . , 1453).

[3] Eight hundred "milliers" (*Inventaire des Archives Communales de Périgueux*, EE21). Cf. Archives communales de Pézenas, no. 1728, charte no. 39.

It was a method admirably adapted to the logical system of administration which the king's ministers were building up, with the entire realm divided and subdivided into manageable administrative units, all governed by officers whose power was derived directly or indirectly from the fountain-head of authority in the Louvre.

With the growth of royal absolutism, the French kings increased their efforts to root out the illicit manufacture of saltpetre, gunpowder, and artillery pieces by persons who held no royal commissions, and to prevent the export of these munitions for the use of the king's enemies. The most important royal enactments dealing with these matters were passed in 1572, 1582, and 1601.[4] The ordinance of 1601 declared that the right to make saltpetre and gun-powder was as much an attribute of sovereignty as the right to coin money. Persons making ammunition without royal authority were criminals, like counterfeiters, punishable by death and by confiscation of the plant and the tools they had used. In addition any person who manufactured powder without a royal commission was to be fined fifty *livres* for every pound, or more than a hundred times its value.[5] The management of the royal saltpetre and gunpowder manufacture was placed in the hands of the grand master of the artillery.[6] From 1599 until 1610 this office was occupied by the great Sully himself, Henri IV's principal minister, whose genius as an administrator was equalled only by that of Colbert. He applied to the control of the munitions industries no less skill and devotion to the royal service than he showed during the same years in managing the national finances for the king. The ordinance of 1601 revoked all commissions for manufacturing ammunition that had not been granted by Sully during the three previous years. He and his agents were given the exclusive right to grant new

[4] See recitals in Archives Nationales, X1A8663, ff. 350–3.

[5] At Riom in 1632, the municipal authorities paid only fifty and sixty *livres* for a cwt. of gunpowder (Archives communales de Riom, HH2, no. 1878. See below, p. 64).

[6] Archives Nationales, X1A8644, ff. 380–3 (partly printed in *Recueil général des anciennes lois françaises*, Paris, 1829, vol. xv, pp. 263–6).

commissions, and it was stated in the ordinance that whenever one grand master was succeeded by another, the commissions of his predecessor should be void until they were renewed. Every bit of saltpetre or gunpowder made by authorized producers had to be placed in the royal storehouses. Even private persons who needed powder for shooting game in the woods and prairies near their homes, were obliged to buy it from the royal storehouses at prices, fixed by the government [7] and on days appointed by the grand master.

In spite of Sully's administrative genius, in spite of the ardor of some of his agents, and in spite of the special edicts passed to supplement the ordinance of 1601 in particular towns and districts, a good deal of gunpowder was still made outside the royal monopoly at places like Le Puy and Montpellier in southern France.[8] But the contraband traffic in ammunition never caused Sully or his successors to falter in their determination to build up a successful manufacture in the king's own hands. After the death of Louis XIII in 1643, the quarrels between the various factions in the civil wars of the Fronde increased the illicit manufacture of gunpowder. Unlike the civil wars in England, these quarrels were not accompanied by the collapse of the royal armament monopoly. In 1663 Louis XIV issued an ordinance insisting upon the enforcement of the earlier enactments of Henri IV and his predecessors.[9] As royal absolutism was more firmly established then ever in the second half of the seventeenth century, and as the king's provincial administration was more efficient, the grand masters of the artillery were in a better position than their predecessors under Henri IV and Louis XIII to control the making of munitions.

The grand master's control did not consist simply in his power to grant or revoke commissions to private persons, permitting them to collect saltpetre earth to convert into

7 Cf. Archives communales de Riom, HH2, no. 1878.

8 Archives Nationales, E4B, f. 342; E12A, f. 16r°. See also *Inventaire des Archives départementales des Bouches-du-Rhône*, B3343, f. 701v°.

9 Archives Nationales, X1A8663, ff. 350–3. Cf. Archives départementales de l'Hérault, B8 (*Déclaration*, October, 1699).

saltpetre and then into gunpowder. Under him a hierarchy of officials concerned themselves with the manufacture and transport of powder. At least as early as Henri IV's reign, royal commissioners for saltpetre and gunpowder were appointed in the provinces. It was the business of these officers to decide where, when, and by whom saltpetre should be manufactured, where, when, and by whom powder mills and drying rooms should be built. It was also their business to provide capital, equipment, and tools for the manufacturers to build and repair arsenals and magazines for storing ammunition, and to pay for the saltpetre and gunpowder when it was delivered at the storehouses. If the commissioners were not on the spot and able to treat directly with the producers, they appointed agents to act for them. In many towns the municipal governments, which were increasingly controlled by the king,[10] acted as agents for the commissioners. As agents they entered into contracts with local petre and powder makers. Sometimes the same master workman made both petre and powder. More frequently the saltpetre makers delivered the petre they made to the royal storehouses, and the king's officers or their agents turned it over to local powder makers who came to fetch it.

In the mountains of Auvergne, at Riom, at least as early as 1574, the manufacture of saltpetre and gunpowder was managed for the royal service by the municipal governors, the consuls, with the help of the king's counsel (*conseiller du roi*) and the public prosecutor from the district court (*siège présidial*).[11] The same system was in force sixty years later at this town of some 6,000 or 7,000 people. In 1632 when the office of first consul, or mayor, was held by the king's counsel, the municipal government entered into a contract for stores of ammunition with two saltpetre makers from the nearby bourg of Chantelle. One of the saltpetre makers agreed to bring his family to Riom, where he was to live for the rest of his life, without paying rent, in the saltpetre house owned by the town. This house, which had been

10 See above, p. 36.
11 Archives communales de Riom, HH2, nos. 657, 660, 661.

the home of earlier saltpetre makers, was equipped with the kettles, basins, and tools needed for the manufacture. The two saltpetre makers agreed to leave the equipment in as good condition as they found it. They were also to receive an advance of 150 *écus* from the municipal governors to build a gunpowder mill, which was to become the property of the town. In return for the right to use the house and mill, the saltpetre makers agreed to deliver stipulated quantities of gunpowder to the consuls every year at prices of fifty and sixty *livres* a hundredweight.[12]

Two and a half years later one of these saltpetre men entered into another contract with François Sabatier, the commissioner general for gunpowder and saltpetre in France, who usually dealt with the producers through his agents. Under the new contract, the saltpetre man at Riom agreed to deliver half a ton of powder annually to the royal arsenal at Lyons, a distance of more than a hundred miles through steep hills.[13] At about the same time an agent of Sabatier's in southwestern France, at the little town of Gramat in Quercy, made a contract with two saltpetre makers, one from Lisle-sur-Tarn, the other from Rouerque. Sabatier's agent undertook to send a copper kettle weighing 190 pounds sixty miles to Montauban, where these master workmen were to set up their shop. They agreed to pay him an annual rent of a hundredweight of saltpetre for the use of the kettle. As at Riom, the two saltpetre men formed a partnership for the manufacture.[14] With the help of capital supplied directly by the royal commissioners or by their agents, shops for making saltpetre were set up all over the country.[15]

12 Archives communales de Riom, HH2, no. 1878.

13 *Ibid.*

14 Archives départementales du Tarn, E576, ff. 44–6 (Bibliothèque Municipale, Albi).

15 For a similar arrangement in connection with the manufacture of saltpetre at Narbonne, see Archives départementales de l'Hérault, A46. For Libourne, Archives départementales de la Gironde, E. suppl. 4411 (BB8). For Crécy-sur-Serre, near Laon in Picardy, Archives départementales de l'Aisne, B503.

The saltpetre makers were granted a number of privileges by the king and the grand master of the artillery. In nearby towns and villages they were given the right to search for saltpetre earth in ruins, barns, cellars, bird houses, cattle sheds, and even in dwellings, and to take what they found without paying the owners. The king was claiming regalian rights to saltpetre in the lands of his subjects, just as he was claiming regalian rights to the ores under the lands of his subjects. The only restriction was that the right of search, in some cases at any rate, did not extend to the buildings of the nobility and the clergy.[16] If the saltpetre men found a house bolted that they were entitled to enter, and if the owner refused to open it, they were authorized in some cases to go to the nearest locksmith and have him make them a key. In addition to the right of search, the saltpetre men could commandeer workmen, horses, and harnesses to help them carry their materials, paying a reasonable sum for hire. Everywhere, in Picardy and Provence, in Auvergne and Languedoc, they were given permission to collect dead wood in the royal forests free of charge, to provide them with the fuel they needed in their manufacture.[17] Gunpowder makers were sometimes authorized directly by the council of state to cut oaks from the royal forests to repair their mills and their drying rooms.[18] Like almost all the workers in the royal and privileged manufactures, the saltpetre and gunpowder makers were exempted, along with the nobles and the clergy, from paying the *taille*.[19]

The money needed to provide the manufacturing plant and equipment, to pay the contractors, and to carry powder from one town to another was generally supplied out of the

[16] Archives départementales des Bouches-du-Rhône, dépôts d'Aix, B3353, f. 165v°.

[17] Archives départementales de l'Aisne, B503; Bouches-du-Rhône, Dépôts d'Aix, B3353, f. 165v°; Archives communales de Riom, HH2, no. 657, 1878; Archives départementales du Tarn, E576, f. 79.

[18] Bibliothèque Nationale, MSS. français, 18165, f. 485v°.

[19] Archives communales de Riom, HH2, no. 1878.

king's revenue collected in the provinces.[20]   Sometimes the
costs were met out of the proceeds from a particular tax.
That was the way the king's ministers paid Nicholas de
Corberon, commissioner for saltpetre and gunpowder in
Champagne and Burgundy in the reign of Henri IV.   Corberon maintained a powder mill and magazine at Troyes
under a contract he had entered into with the council of
state.[21]   In 1597 he was granted the right to take the pay-
ments due him by the crown for deliveries of powder out of
the receipts from the *taille* collected at Troyes.[22]   Later, toward the end of Louis XIII's reign, various provinces and
towns were asked to raise special funds every year toward
the manufacture of saltpetre.[23]   In 1635 the council of state
decreed that the province of Languedoc should pay 30,000
livres in 1636, and 10,000 *livres* annually thereafter for this
purpose.[24]

Before the death of Louis XIII, in 1643, the manufacture
of ammunition in France had been firmly established as a
vast royal enterprise, consisting mainly of a large number
of local units, managed by private contractors, dependent
for their privileges and for a large part of their capital
upon the king's agents.[25]   The powder mills, like the saltpetre shops, were generally small, frequently no larger than
the ancient flour mills, which were sometimes remodeled and
adapted for the new manufacture.[26]   While the English
monarchs usually depended for their supplies of powder
upon a few large mills near London, operated as one enterprise by a single contractor, generally a member of the rich
Evelyn family, the French kings received a large portion of

[20] Archives Nationales, E1B, ff. 85, 117, 192; Bibliothèque Nationale,
MSS. français, 18160, ff. 89v°–90.

[21] *Ibid.*, 18165, f. 485v°.

[22] *Ibid.*, 18160, f. 5v°.

[23] Cf. *Inventaire des Archives communales, Bourg-en-Bresse*, HH13.

[24] Archives départementales de l'Hérault, A44.

[25] Arrangements similar to those made in the saltpetre and gunpowder
industries were made for the manufacture of supplies of artillery (*Inventaire
des Archives départementales du Gard*, E, vol. ii, pp. 223, 232).

[26] Archives départementales de l'Hérault, A46 (*Contrat . . . pour le ré-
édification d'un moulin,* 1621).

their supplies in driblets from scores of little mills scattered all over France. At the time when the two master workmen at Riom were bound to deliver only about a ton of powder a year, half at Riom and half at Lyons,[27] the king's powder maker in England was under contract to send annually to the Tower of London 240 tons.[28] In southern France the powder makers who entered into contracts with the king's agents were generally humble craftsmen like the local weavers, leather makers, and smiths. An inventory taken by a notary in 1626, after the death of one such powder maker at Barjols, a place with perhaps 2,000 inhabitants, thirty-five miles east of Aix-en-Provence, shows us a man of very small substance. Meixemin Merlle left behind him in his tiny cottage one foul bed, two much-worn coats, four plates and three spoons, besides some crude furniture. In the room where he made his powder were a few tools, two scales, and an old arquebus. In addition he left some grain growing in the fields, for he had held a bit of land as tenant of a magistrate in the court of the *bailliage,* who lived at Brignoles, a slightly larger place some miles to the south. Merlle's property was hardly worth enough to cover the debts of seventy-eight *livres* five *sous,* or about £ 6 sterling, which he owed in small amounts to fifteen of his fellow townsmen.[29]

It was men of little greater wealth than Merlle who entered into contracts with the king's agents in many other towns as master saltpetre and master powder makers. Even when the grand master of the king's artillery drew up a contract for a large supply of powder, the manufacture was often parcelled out among many separate producers. In 1601 Sully gave a military commander of Montpellier, named Michel Vivens, charge of all powder production for the whole of the great province of Languedoc.[30] Evidently Vivens did not concentrate the manufacture at any one

[27] Archives communales de Riom, HH2, no. 1878.

[28] Nef, ''A Comparison of Industrial Growth in France and England,'' p. 647.

[29] Archives départementales du Var, E1133, ff. 416–19.

[30] Archives départementales de l'Hérault, B29.

place, for twenty years later a part of the powder supply of the province came from several small mills in the west, at Béziers and Narbonne.[31] At Marseilles, the largest town in Provence, gunpowder was still made by four separate manufacturers even as late as 1684. Two of them had establishments built on the canals, about thirty-two feet long and twenty-eight feet wide, no larger than an ordinary bedroom in the castle of a nobleman.[32] Without the large and efficient provincial administration built up under the French kings, and the special royal officers who devoted themselves to the royal manufacture of ammunition, it would have been impossible for the crown to maintain its control of such dispersed industries as saltpetre and gunpowder making.

The Mining and Metallurgical Industries in France.

The control established by the crown over mining and metallurgy was of a different sort, because the kings did not try to handle all the base ores and minerals produced in the realm, as they tried to handle all the saltpetre and gunpowder. By a series of ordinances, edicts, and letters patent, they asserted their right to a revenue from ores and minerals. This right rested on the ancient *droit de dixième* (derived perhaps from Roman imperial law), according to which the sovereign was entitled to a part of the produce of all mines. An edict of 1413 had laid it down as a principle that the king of France had the exclusive right to this royalty as over against all other overlords, lay and ecclesiastical, some of whom had been collecting it.[33] In the fifteenth century the right of landlords to take minerals and ores from underneath their fiefs and lordships, provided they paid the *dixième,* does not appear to have been seriously challenged. It was not yet a settled principle of French law that mines throughout the kingdom were at the disposal of the crown, although an edict of 1471 required landlords

[31] *Ibid.,* C (*Délibérations des Etats de Languedoc,* 1620–22) and A46.

[32] Archives départementales des Bouches-du-Rhône, C2185, ff. 475–84.

[33] *Recueil général des anciennes lois françaises,* Paris, 1825, vol. vii, pp. 386–90.

to notify the royal officials within forty days of the discovery of minerals under their territory, and to begin preparations for mining within the three following months, under pain of losing their title to the ore.[34]

In the sixteenth century the pretensions of the French kings in connection with mines were pushed further than in the past. After 1540 they seem to have claimed as an attribute of sovereignty the power to dispose of mines under private lands, as the Hohenstauffen emperors had done in the twelfth century. Unlike some of the German territorial princes, who acquired sovereign rights in various parts of the Holy Roman Empire during the later Middle Ages, the French kings succeeded in extending their regalian claims to ores and minerals of every description. Their method of getting mines worked differed from that common in medieval times in Germany and central Europe. Instead of throwing mining open to all comers and granting tiny concessions (of a small part of a seam of ore) to the finder and to other applicants, they granted large general concessions. Between 1548 and 1640 scores of such concessions, for limited terms of years, were made to court favorites and others.[35] The king conceded the right to mine various ores and minerals, including iron ore frequently and coal occasionally, in the kingdom as a whole, or in certain provinces, or in particular localities.[36] These concessions often over-

[34] P. Boissonnade, *Le socialisme d'état*, Paris, 1927, pp. 63–4; *Recueil général des anciennes lois françaises*, vol. x, pp. 626–7.

[35] The first of these concessions was the celebrated one made September 30, 1548, for a period of nine years, to Jean François de la Rocque, seigneur de Roberval, an explorer who had been associated with Jacques Cartier in his voyages to Canada (Archives Nationales, K171, no. 25; cf. *ibid.*, X1A8624, ff. 271–7—printed in *Recueil général des anciennes lois françaises*, vol. xiii, pp. 57–60). For the history of this concession after Roberval's death, see Archives départementales de la Haute-Garonne, B. Lettre Patente, Régistre viii, ff. 116v° sqq.; Boissonnade, *op. cit.*, p. 68. The policy of granting mining concessions was not new. But the older concessions were usually limited to mines containing precious metal.

[36] If, as the words of the original letters patent of 1548 to Roberval suggest, Henri II intended to create a monopoly of all kinds of mining in the hands of one group of concessionaires ("nul autre que le dit Roberval, . . . les siens, commis et associés, n'ayant semblablement privilèges précédents en

lapped, so that more than one group of concessionaires held a title to mine at one time in the same territory.[37]   But there was seldom any serious conflict between such groups.   We have no evidence of pitched battles fought by their miners with picks and shovels.   So many of the efforts to discover new seams of ore were half-hearted, and so many others gave disappointing results, that a concessionaire rarely had any cause to envy his rivals.

By granting concessions the royal officials hoped to stimulate the search for new mines and to increase the national output of minerals and metals.   At the same time, the concessions provided the king with a means of asserting his claim to the ownership of all subterranean wealth and his right to a revenue from the produce of all mines.   In one of the concessions, in 1564, the king's ownership was said to extend to all ''mines, metallurgic and non-metallurgic matter, and all underground substances hidden in the interior of the earth''.[38]   Over and over again it was stated that the king's concessionaires could mine, build furnaces, forges, and mills of all kinds for converting ore into metal,

datte ces présentes, puissent faire aucune ouverture des dites mines''—Archives Nationales, K171, no. 25), such a project was abandoned after his death in 1559, if not before (Archives départementales de la Haute-Garonne, B. Lettres Patentes, Régistre viii, ff. 116v° sqq., 225 sqq.; cf. Archives Nationales, X1A8634, ff. 314v°–5; Archives départementales des Bouches-du-Rhône, B3331, f. 680; B3332, f. 664).   In 1560 the seigneur de Lafayette was granted the privilege to mine in his lands of Pontgibaud, near Clermont-Ferrand.   He had obtained a concession earlier, in 1554, to build forges for smelting silver and copper ore (*Inventaire sommaire des Archives départementales du Doubs*, série B, vol. iii (1895), p. 157).   An ordinance of 1579 indicates that all subjects skilled in mining were entitled to apply to the crown for the right to mine anywhere, except under towns, churches, castles, and other important buildings (Archives Nationales, X1A8634, f. 482).   At the beginning of the seventeenth century we find several concessionaires simultaneously holding letters patent or other privileges permitting them to mine all kinds of ores and minerals throughout the realm (Archives Nationales, X1A8644, ff. 390–5, 400–5; Archives départementales des Bouches-du-Rhône, B3342, f. 211v°), while still others had the right to mine at specified places (Archives départementales des Bouches-du-Rhône, B3344, f. 1021v°).

[37] E.g., Archives départementales de la Haute-Garonne, B. Lettres Patentes, Régistre viii, ff. 208–10, 225 sqq.

[38] Archives Nationales, X1A8625, ff. 274–5.

and make paths for carrying wood, charcoal, and ore in the land of any subject. They had to pay the landlord reasonable compensation if they damaged his property. The amount was fixed by local judges. The concessionaires were not to pay anything for the ores or minerals which they took.

It was the king who was to be paid for the ores and minerals. He was to receive a revenue, except when by royal enactment he voluntarily renounced it. The principle is stated very clearly in an edict of 1563. "We hearby declare," runs the royal enactment, "that the *droit de dixième* is ours by sovereign right on all mines which have been or shall be opened at whatever time and by whatever hands in our entire kingdom. . . ." [39]

If the crown was to get a revenue from the mines, the king had to do more than assert by ordinance, edict, and letters patent his right to it. Administrative machinery for collecting it had to be built up and perfected. A national administration for mines had been created by the Valois kings during the fifteenth century.[40] In Henri IV's reign this administration was extended and strengthened by three edicts of 1597, 1601, and 1604. At the head of the new administration was a general superintendent (*the surintendant et réformateur général des mines*). A number of permanent salaried officials were appointed to assist him in collecting revenue, granting concessions, settling disputes, caring for the workmen, and providing expert technical advice. During the first half of the seventeenth century the number of these officials was increased.[41] Before 1640 fifteen *lieutenants particuliers* were added, each of whom had control of the mining administration in one or more provinces. With a force of thirty handsomely-paid major officers, aided by assistants, it was a comparatively easy matter to enforce

[39] This version is from Archives départementales des Bouches-du-Rhône, B3331, f. 681. The version in the Archives Nationales (X1A8625, ff. 44–5) is essentially the same.

[40] Boissonnade, *op. cit.*, p. 65.

[41] *Ibid.*, pp. 216–8; Archives Nationales, X1A8644, ff. 400–5.

the mining regulations of the national government, and to collect the revenue due the king from mines.[42]

On its face the *droit de dixième* was a claim to a tenth of the produce from mining operations. But the amount actually collected by the king's officials was not the same for all ores. In 1601 we find the crown claiming a fifth on gold, a tenth on silver, and a fifteenth on copper and less valuable ores and minerals.[43] In the same year Henri IV voluntarily relinquished his royalty on coal, but he did it in such a way as not to prejudice the claim of the crown that the right to dispose of coal seams, like the right to dispose of seams of other minerals, was an attribute of sovereignty.[44] No attempt was apparently made to tax the iron ore at the place where it was extracted from the earth.[45] The crown was asserting its right, in theory, to the possession of all ores and minerals and to the management of all mining enterprises, but, in practice, the royal mining administration concerned itself almost entirely with large enterprises for digging and smelting the more valuable ores. Nearly all the coal and iron ore obtained in France was dug by small groups of local peasants, sometimes on their own initiative, sometimes with the help of capital advanced by local landlords or town merchants. The peasants usually went to work without any authorization from the crown and without any agreement with the holders of the royal mining concessions. They were seldom bothered by the king's officials or by the concessionaires, who were usually searching only for gold, silver, copper, lead, tin, or alum. The great number of tiny enterprises for digging iron ore made it impracticable for the crown to collect a revenue at the mines. The

[42] We have the account book of the royal mining administration for 1640. The salaries of the chief officials ranged from 4,000 to 8,000 *livres* per annum (Archives Nationales, KK509).

[43] Archives Nationales, X1A8644, ff. 400–5. When gold was a by-product of some other ore, the king was apparently entitled to a larger percentage of it than a fifth.

[44] Marcel Rouff, *Les mines de charbon en France,* Paris, 1922, p. xvi.

[45] Nevertheless we find a certain Jean Ponthoise offering in 1608 to pay the crown 20,000 *livres* a year for the right to farm the *droit de dixième* on all mines of iron ore and coal (Archives Nationales, E18B, fol. 259, i).

furnaces and forges at which the ore was smelted were generally considerably larger enterprises, run by adventurers who could be held responsible much more easily than the peasants who supplied them with the ore. As was common in central Europe during the later Middle Ages, among those princes whose regalian rights extended to iron ore, the revenue was collected, not at the mines, but at the smelting works.

By a royal edict of 1542 the owners of forges in Burgundy were required to pay a *livre tournois* on every thousandweight of iron, approximately half a ton. The *livre,* at the time, was worth about two English shillings, and we have to multiply those shillings by at least twelve to get their equivalent in modern money. This was apparently one of the first attempts by the crown to levy a considerable tax on the produce of iron forges. Anthoine Brocard, a member of the chamber of accounts at Dijon, has left behind a record of the steps he took to enforce the edict in the *bailliage* of Auxois. He first journeyed to Semur-en-Auxois, that marvelous hill town which today is still untouched by the railroad and which retains the wonderful harmony of design it inherited from the Middle Ages and the Renaissance. There he consulted the local *lieutenant-général* (who represented the king), the mayor, and two iron merchants. They told him no tax had been previously levied on iron in the *bailliage*. He then visited the one forge which was said to be in operation, and interviewed the master and various workmen, whom he obliged to testify under oath. They confirmed the testimony of the officials and merchants of Semur. No one connected with the iron industry had yet heard of the edict. Monsieur Brocard told them that henceforth the tax must be paid into the hands of the crown officials of the *bailliage*. They unanimously professed their willingness to conform to the king's orders. Monsieur Brocard also visited La Buzière, a place with an abandoned forge belonging to an abbey, and warned the local monks that the abbot, absent at the time, must conform to the new regulations if he again made iron. At

Semur, Saulieu, and Arnay-le-Duc, the chief towns in the *bailliage*, Monsieur Brocard ordered the local officials to read out to the people the new edict and to post it in a prominent place for all to see.[46]

If, as seems possible, equally conscientious officials took the matter in hand in other *bailliages*, it must have been difficult in Burgundy to escape payment of the new imposition. Until 1543, the tax of a *livre* per thousandweight had been levied only in certain regions, but in that year an ordinance was passed extending it to all iron produced in France, and making the masters of the forges responsible for its payment.[47] The tax was increased before the end of the sixteenth century. In 1626 it amounted to five *livres* a thousandweight on bar iron.[48] The increase at least covered the fall on the value of money. The growth of a strong mining administration in the provinces facilitated the collection of the tax. An attempt was even made in the thirties, when Richelieu controlled the financial administration, to exact a payment from the ironmasters in Brittany, a province which claimed almost complete independence of the crown in matters of taxation.[49] By 1640 the account book kept by the mining administration shows that the tax on iron was bringing into the royal treasury 72,000 *livres,* or some 6,000 pounds sterling.[50]

Poor in most of the more valuable ores, France abounds in iron ore. In the sixteenth and seventeenth centuries the value of iron produced within the realm may have exceeded the value of all other metals combined. The partial success of the crown in establishing its claim to a revenue from iron, shows how effectively the royal officers exercised their

[46] Archives départementales de la Côte d'Or, B11688.

[47] Archives Nationales, X1A8614, ff. 22–3.

[48] Archives Nationales, X1A8650, ff. 328–34. The tax was levied on the hundredweight, 20 *sous* the cwt. of steel, 10 *sous* the cwt. of bar iron, 6 *sous*, 8 *deniers* the cwt. of pig iron (*ibid.*, KK509).

[49] Archives départementales d'Ille-et-Vilaine, C2771.

[50] Archives Nationales, KK509. In 1644 the tax brought in 79,818 *livres,* 15 *sous*, and in 1654, 92,000 *livres* (*ibid.*, KK510, KK511). For the relation between the *livre tournois* and the pound sterling, see below, pp. 126, n., 128, n.

power over mining and metallurgical enterprise during the hundred years preceding the accession of Louis XIV, in 1643.

Everywhere the mining of the more valuable ores came to be subject to royal regulation.[51] A decree of 1604 provided a code of rules for the miners and the owners of mines. The king's officials were expected, among other things, to look after the morals of the workmen. Miners who swore or played illicit games were to be punished. It was an age when the French kings, like most other continental princes, still assumed that the crown, along with the church, had a responsibility for the morality of its subjects. Only in England, and perhaps in Holland, was there already a tendency to take the view which was to dominate in late nineteenth-century Europe, that private morals were a matter for individual taste, to be allowed to take care of themselves except in criminal cases. One-thirtieth of all profits from mines was to be paid to one of the royal officers, the general treasurer, to constitute a fund out of which one or two priests and a surgeon were to be paid for looking after the spiritual welfare and the health of the workers at each enterprise. No entrepreneur could abandon mining operations without first informing the chief of the royal administration. None of the king's mining officials were allowed to hold an interest in any mines.[52]

By these and other provisions the crown established a sort of protectorate over the principal mining enterprises, modelled to some extent after the mining administrations of sovereign lords in Germany and central Europe. Nearly all of the large mines were in the hands of concessionaires dependent for their success partly upon royal favors, granting them permission to manage the mines without losing their status as nobles, exempting their workmen from paying the *taille* and other direct taxes, and allowing them to

[51] See, e.g., Archives départementales des Bouches-du-Rhône, B3341, f. 595 (1602).
[52] Archives Nationales, AD¹138, no. 11.

bring in, and after a time to naturalize, skilled miners from foreign countries.[53]

While the royal officials did not attempt such an extensive regulation of iron furnaces and forges, the ordinance of 1543, which extended the tax on iron to all forges in the realm, also declared that, in the interest of conserving the wood supplies, the number of iron mills should not be increased.[54] Henceforth no new forge was to be started without the permission of the crown or of the provincial *parlement*.[55] When a landlord wanted to lease a portion of his land to an ironmaster, or on his own account to build and equip plant for smelting iron ore or slitting iron, one or more of the king's provincial officials were generally asked to determine whether the establishment would be of benefit to the public.[56] If they gave a favorable report, the landlord or his lessee could generally get permission from the crown, either by letters patent or by decree of the king's council, to build mills and forges, to dig for ore and to cut wood for fuel.[57]

The Making of Salt in France.

The control established by the crown over salt making was no less effective than the control established over mining and metallurgy, and it yielded the royal treasury an overwhelmingly greater financial return. At a time when kings and princes all over Europe were at their wit's ends to know how to make their revenues keep pace with their expenditures, the revenue obtained by the French crown from salt was so large as to be of fundamental importance for the maintenance of the royal authority. In many provinces the crown had established a claim to a tax on salt during the fourteenth and fifteenth centuries. This tax was

[53] Archives Nationales, X1A8644, fols. 400v°–5; Archives départementales de la Haute-Garonne, B. Lettres Patentes, Régistre no. 8, ff. 208–10.

[54] Archives Nationales, X1A8614, ff. 22–3.

[55] Boissonnade, *op. cit.*, p. 74; Hauser, *Les débuts du capitalisme*, p. 122. Cf. Hauser, *Ouvriers du temps passé*, 5th ed., p. 256.

[56] See, e.g., Archives départementales de la Côte d'Or, B12101, f. 214v°.

[57] Cf. Boissonnade, *op. cit.*, pp. 231–2.

called the *gabelle*. It was collected by means of a royal monopoly of the sale of salt, which was stored by order of the crown in royal storehouses built in nearly all large towns and in some villages throughout France. All traders who obtained salt from the marshes along the Mediterranean and the Bay of Biscay, or from the brine springs of Franche-Comté, were expected to bring it to these storehouses. There it was placed in rooms under triple lock and key. One of the keys was given to the trader. One was given to each of the two royal officials in charge of the storehouse—the *grénetier* and the *contrôleur du grénetier*. No salt brought to the storehouses could be sold to the public without the knowledge of both these officers.

In addition to his claim to the *gabelle,* the king had in Languedoc an older title as feudal lord to a share in the produce of certain salt marshes. His title covered the most important ones in southern France, those at Peccais, near the famous old town of Aigues-Mortes, with its thirteenth-century fortifications.[58] In Languedoc the *gabelle* came to be regarded as part of the king's regalian rights, similar to the *droit de dixième,* which entitled him to a share of the produce of ores and minerals. It also corresponded to the tribute which had been levied on salt by the imperial Roman state.[59]

During the fifteenth century the crown had called in the services of semi-official organizations of private traders to help the royal officers in supplying the storehouses and in managing the sale of salt. This policy had not produced the desired result. In Languedoc revenue from the *gabelle* declined. At the beginning of the fifteenth century it

[58] Ed. Meynial, ''Etudes sur la gabelle du sel avant le XVIIᵉ siècle en France,'' *Tijdschrift voor Rechtsgeschiedenis,* Haarlem, vol. iii (1921), vol. iv (1922). For the rights of the king in Languedoc, see vol. iii, pp. 159–61; vol. iv, p. 134. Cf. Jules Finot, *Essai historique sur les origines de la gabelle,* Lons-le-Saunier, 1866, pp. 27–31.

[59] Archives départementales de l'Hérault, Fonds de Sézieux, *Mémoire de Lamoignon de Basville,* Intendant de Languedoc. I owe my knowledge of this document to M. de Dainville and M. Maury, who kindly made a copy for me.

amounted to some 90,000 *livres tournois* a year. A hundred years later, in 1497, when the value of French money was somewhat less than in 1400, the receipts were only 53,938 *livres tournois*.[60] Private traders had become increasingly bold about selling salt outside the royal monopoly for their own advantage, as their connections with the crown administration made it easy for them to do.[61]

Louis XII and Francis I determined to rid the royal administration of these private interests. Edicts passed in 1508 and 1517 show that the crown had ceased to rely on the help of private traders in collecting the *gabelle*. Between 1541 and 1547 the whole question of its administration was reconsidered. Letters patent aimed to do away with all free trade in salt; they reasserted the right of the royal officials to a monopoly of the sale.[62] Francis I's attempt to root out the frauds practiced at the salt marshes in southwestern France led to an armed insurrection in 1541 and 1542, and caused the king to confiscate a number of marshes between Bordeaux and La Rochelle.[63] The struggle over the collection of the tax in the southwest was finally settled in 1549 and 1553, when a large group of provinces, including Poitou, Saintonge, Aunis, Angoumois, and Périgord purchased perpetual exemption for 1,743,500 *livres*. Brittany also was left outside the territory subject to the *gabelle*. Elsewhere the authority of the royal officials who controlled the salt trade grew greatly during the hundred years following 1541.

Unlike the brine salt works in Franche-Comté and Lorraine, most of the salt marshes along the French coasts were in private hands, but the owners' business was so extensively regulated by the royal officials that they had little freedom of enterprise. Like the makers of saltpetre and gunpowder, they were obliged to sell their product to the

[60] Meynial, *op. cit.*, vol. iv, pp. 165–6.

[61] Edward Hughes, *Studies in Administration and Finance, 1558–1825*, Manchester, 1934, p. 16; G. Dupont-Ferrier, *Etudes sur les institutions financières de la France à la fin du moyen âge*, Paris, 1932, vol. ii, pp. 128–9.

[62] Hughes, *op. cit.*, pp. 16–7.

[63] Archives Nationales, X1A8613, ff. 444–5.

royal storehouses at prices fixed by the king's officers. These officers specified the quantity which the owners of the marshes might sell, and the government storehouses to which the produce must be brought. The owners were sometimes allowed to sell directly to foreign traders, but they had to pay the crown a heavy tax on all salt that was exported.[64] Rigorous measures were taken to prevent the purchase of any salt by private persons at the marshes, or anywhere except at the royal storehouses.[65] In western Normandy, where salt was made from sea water in tiny quantities all along the coast from Caen to Mont-Saint-Michel, it was easier for local landlords to evade the royal regulations and acquire stores of contraband salt than in provinces like Languedoc and Provence, where production was concentrated in a few centers. Some of their estates were conveniently situated for smuggling in salt from Brittany, where there was no regulation of the trade. In 1599 a commission was appointed to visit western Normandy and try to put an end to the extensive illicit traffic in salt. The commissioners were given the right to ransack the houses of landlords suspected of having hidden stores to dispose of to their tenants, who were frequently dependent on them for their supplies of salt and other necessary commodities, such as cider, wine, or beer. The offenders were to be summoned to Rouen before the *Cour des Aides,* which had jurisdiction in tax cases. Other extraordinary measures were undertaken to put a stop to the contraband salt traffic in western Normandy, and to call to account public officials who, like the *gouverneur* of Pontorson on the border of Brittany, were suspected of abetting bands of salt smugglers in nearby villages. Similar efforts to stamp out smuggling were made in eastern Normandy, at the mouth of the Seine, in Touraine, and throughout the country.[66]

[64] See, e.g., Archives Nationales, E21, ff. 275 sqq.

[65] See, e.g., the royal decrees, Archives Nationales, E4B, ff. 97r°, 434; E10A, f. 77.

[66] Archives Nationales, E2A, fol. 121; E15B, f. 82; E19B, f. 262; E24C, ff. 489, 496, 498.

The cultivation of salt at the marshes in southern France was controlled by the crown in a variety of ways. In 1600 the king's officials ordered the flooding of a number of small marshes along the coasts of Languedoc. Thus they managed to concentrate all production at Peccais, where the crown as overlord had a direct interest in the salt produced, and where its transport to specified storehouses could be easily supervised.[67] The great Sully, as the king's chief minister, found it worth while to indemnify the owners of the flooded saltworks for abstaining from production.[68] Evidently the idea of having the national government pay producers for "ploughing under" their crops is no new device of our own time.

In Provence the chief marshes were at Hyères, now a famous watering place on the Riviera, and at Berre, a town on the great pond near the mouth of the Rhône. For the establishment of new marshes or the enlargement of old ones, the king's permission was needed, and he left it to the provincial officials in charge of the royal revenue to decide whether the proposed additions were in the public interest.[69]

The ease with which the king's councillors in Paris could get prompt and reliable reports on local economic conditions from the royal officials in the provinces, greatly facilitated the efficient regulation of revenue-yielding industries like mining, metallurgy, and salt making. Requests for information and advice could be despatched to Aix-en-Provence, to Montpellier, or to Poitiers, with a confidence in the accuracy and in the loyalty of the replies, which the

[67] Archives départementales de l'Hérault, B28: Archives Nationales, E14A, fol. 29; Boissonnade, *op. cit.*, p. 228. The marshes at Peyriac and Sigean, near Narbonne, were exempted from the order closing down the salt works which competed with Peccais, and a royal decree of 1605 permitted the revival of certain small enterprises along the coast in case the yield at Peccais proved insufficient to supply the markets (Archives Nationales, E8B, fol. 155). But Peccais seems to have provided most of the salt made in Languedoc during the seventeenth century, at least until 1691, when a decree of the council of state stipulated that salt for upper Languedoc should come from the marshes near Narbonne and not from Peccais (Archives départementales de l'Hérault, Fonds de Sézieux, *Mémoire de Basville*).

[68] Archives Nationales, E14A, fol. 29.

[69] Archives Nationales, E6B, f. 120; E8A, f. 28.

English king and his ministers could not always feel in the reports they got from local commissioners or justices of the peace, who were less disinterested and who had less time to devote to royal business than French officials. These officials, in their turn, were in continual correspondence with the owners of the large salt marshes both in Languedoc and Provence. They made frequent visits to the marshes. They seem to have known everything that went on there.[70] They left behind detailed accounts of the damage done at the marshes by almost every violent *mistral* which swept down the Rhône valley in the late summers and autumns, to scatter the salt about the adjacent fields and swamps as it lay awaiting carriage to nearby storehouses. The government became more and more deeply involved in salt production, and advanced capital to help the owners of the marshes. In 1598, 10,000 *écus,* about 30,000 *livres tournois,* was appropriated to repair the port of Aigues Mortes, where the ships came for their ladings of Peccais salt.[71]

After the religious wars salt cultivation and the traffic in salt throughout the realm were regulated with great efficiency, by a large number of royal officials, in the interest of the national revenue. During the reign of Henri IV in particular, Sully and his assistants became so zealous about the collection of the *gabelle* that they hoped to prevent even a hogshead of salt from escaping the tax.[72] As time went on the crown succeeded in forcing the inhabitants of hundreds of parishes to purchase more salt every year from the royal storehouses than they had any need for. In this way the smugglers were deprived of their clients, and royal officials were given a free hand to inflate the price of salt to include an increasingly large *gabelle.* Frenchmen were sometimes obliged to pay four times as much for their salt as it would have cost if a free market had existed.

[70] This statement is based on documents too numerous to cite, in the Archives départementales de l'Hérault and des Bouches-du-Rhône.

[71] Bibliothèque Nationale, MSS. français, 18163, ff. 12–3.

[72] This statement is based on a study of the decrees of Henri IV's reign, described in Valois, *op. cit.,* and preserved in the Archives Nationales and the Bibliothèque Nationale.

Why did the people submit to such an exaction? The richer subjects suffered little from the *gabelle,* because many of them were exempt from paying the tax and because, in any case, salt was only a small item in their expenditures. But the great majority of the population—peasants, craftsmen, and small traders—had to cut their savings to the bone and often to suffer acute want in order to take up their quota of salt at inflated prices. If their grumbling did not constitute a serious threat to the power of the crown in the seventeenth century, that was partly because Frenchmen generally, regardless of their social class, were enthusiastically in favor of a strong and even an arbitrary national government as a means of putting an end to the civil dissension of the late sixteenth century. They were accustomed to price fixing by the royal officials in connection with other essential commodities, such as flour and wine. They were accustomed to suffering in a time when their priests taught them that suffering cheerfully borne in this world carried with it the promise of happiness in the next. The priests told them that obedience to the officers of the king, who derived his power from God, was a duty no less urgent than the duty of the servant to obey his master or the duty of the son to obey his father. In his charming little guide to moral Christian conduct, *Introduction à la vie dévote,* written at the beginning of the seventeenth century, St. François de Sales spoke of the sweetness that entered into the performance of these duties. His book was widely read. The priests were everywhere to repeat its lessons. They were far more numerous than the representatives of the Church of England had been since Henry VIII's break with Rome. So the counsel of obedience was more frequently repeated and far more frequently heeded than in England. As the king needed money, and the nation needed the king, the French were prepared to pay a heavy price for order and domestic tranquility, at the very time when English merchants and prominent English gentry, with their growing stakes in capitalistic industry, were coming to regard every tax levied by the crown as trenching on their personal liberties.

As things were in France, the new policy justified the heavy costs which it involved, for the *gabelle,* together with other taxes on salt, became, after the *taille,* the most lucrative source of revenue to the French crown. Between 1523 and 1641 the return in money apparently increased something like forty times over, and in real value eight or ten times over,[73] though the national output of salt did not increase twice over.[74] In 1523 the revenue from the *gabelle* is said to have been about 460,000 *livres tournois.* Some fifty years later, in 1576, the returns had doubled, in spite of the religious wars, which had reduced the production of salt. Three decades later, in 1607, the revenue from the *gabelle* and other taxes on salt was a shade more than six million *livres.* A generation after that, in 1641, on the eve of Richelieu's death, it had risen to almost twenty millions.[75] That was at least twice the annual revenue of the English crown in the decade before the English civil war.[76]

The New Manufactures in France.

The interests of the French kings in industrial enterprises were not confined to the armament industries, mining and metallurgy, and salt making. They came to regard it as their province, especially after the accession of Henri IV, in 1589, to foster new arts and crafts and manufactures,

[73] Prices in France may have risen between 1540 and 1640 as much as fivefold on the average (cf. Nef, ''Prices and Industrial Capitalism in France and England, 1540–1640,'' *Economic History Review,* vol. vii (1937), p. 174).

[74] Nef, ''A Comparison of Industrial Growth in France and England, 1540–1640,'' *Journal of Political Economy,* vol. xliv (1936), p. 298.

[75] J. J. Clamageran, *Histoire de l'impôt en France,* Paris, 1868, vol. ii, pp. 125, 198, 371, 506. Cf. Boissonnade, *op. cit.,* p. 228. Mr. Hughes, citing Monsieur Meynial, gives the figures 53,938 and 91,923 *livres* as the revenue from the *gabelle* for 1497 and 1514 (*op. cit.,* p. 16n.), but these are the figures for Languedoc only (Meynial, *op. cit.,* vol. iv, pp. 164–6). In 1600 the *gabelle* in Languedoc apparently yielded some 400,000 *livres* (Archives départementales de l'Hérault, B28). In 1626 the return was 1,020,000 *livres* (Boissonnade, *op. cit.,* p. 229).

[76] See below, p. 128.

particularly the artistic and the luxury industries, whose products were wanted chiefly to embellish the castles and palaces of the nobility and the royal family.

The rôle played by the crown in introducing such enterprises took various forms. In the first place the king protected inventors by granting them exclusive rights to their inventions for a limited period of ten or twelve, and sometimes as many as twenty-five or thirty years. The earliest patent for an invention of which we have a record was granted in 1551. It gave a courtier named Abel Foulon a ten-year monopoly of his newly-discovered method of making metal type with a geometrical instrument called a holometer.[77] Under Henri IV a much larger number of patents were issued than during the previous forty years.[78] Numerous applicants came to Paris to demonstrate before Sully and his assistants, who then decided whether their methods were novel, successful, and deserving of exclusive privileges.[79] Claude Dangon, a master silk weaver of Lyons, made three special trips to exhibit the brilliantly colored velours he had woven with his newly-invented loom. He was rewarded by a patent, and was granted out of the king's customs collected at Lyons 6,000 *livres* for the patterns he had brought, to enable him to set up twelve looms in his native town.[80] Royal support was not always limited to grants of money. In connection with some patents, the king appointed special royal officers to help the inventors. These officials were paid out of the revenue received from the invention.[81]

As all inventors looked to the crown for support, the royal officials who inspected the inventions helped to determine the direction taken by technological improvement. Sully, Richelieu, and the other leading ministers of Henri IV and Louis XIII did not refuse to grant patents for labor-

[77] Hauser, *Ouvriers du temps passé*, pp. 136–7.

[78] See, e.g., Archives Nationales, X1A8644, ff. 177–9; E1B, ff. 248–9; E6A, f. 330; E8B, f. 201; E18A, ff. 214, 374 sqq.; E24B, f. 256; E24C, f. 133.

[79] *Ibid.*, E24C, ff. 18, 133; E25B, f. 54 sqq.

[80] *Ibid.*, E16B, f. 109.

[81] *Ibid.*, E24C, f. 133.

saving devices when application was made for them. In 1609 two suitors were given the right to introduce the German method of drawing wire with water power in place of hand labor.[82] But the king's advisers were generally looking more for elegant and beautiful results than for machines that would save labor or furnaces that would save fuel. Their influence upon the technical progress of the French nation was thrown more on the side of artistry and quality rather than on that of cheapness and quantity.

A second form of royal intervention concerned the introduction, not of new inventions, but of branches of artistic craftsmanship hitherto practiced only in certain foreign countries. By granting special privileges, the king sought to establish in France the manufacture of the finest glasswares of Venice and Altare, and the manufacture of the finest cloths and tapestries of Italy, Spain, and the Low Countries. The Italians had taken almost as much pains in making glasswares as in painting. In France the king and his advisers were trying to get French craftsmen to emulate the Italian artists.

Sometimes the royal privileges granted to foreigners, or to Frenchmen with special training in the arts, like those granted to inventors, included a monopoly of the manufacture throughout the kingdom.[83] But after the accession of Henri IV, when the granting of privileges became much more common than before, the concessions usually gave their holders exclusive rights only in one or two towns, and sometimes also in the surrounding suburbs and villages.[84] As with mining, so with the artistic industries—the grant of a few general monopolies, especially in the middle decades of the sixteenth century, did not prevent the grant of a much larger number of more limited concessions, especially after the religious wars.

[82] Archives Nationales, E18B, f. 214; E24B, f. 256.

[83] E.g., Archives Nationales, X1A8618, f. 15 (for the making of Venetian glass in 1551); E7A, f. 316 (for the making of gilded leather tapestry in 1604).

[84] E.g., *ibid.*, X1A8643, ff. 59–61; E12A, f. 101; E14A, f. 65; E20A, f. 169; Archives départementales de la Seine-Inférieur, C120, ff. 98–100.

In the places assigned to them, the royal concessionaires were generally given important privileges. All the craftsmen they employed were made independent of the gilds and of the municipal government. Like the gentlemen glass makers in rural areas, where the manufacture of cheap glass commodities had been carried on for centuries, they were exempted from the *taille*. Their wares were not subject to inspection by the local officials.[85] They were directly dependent upon the crown for their right to work. The concessionaires generally received from the government grants of land and sometimes of buildings. One of them, who undertook in the first decade of the seventeenth century to start a new manufacture of fine *crêpes* (*façon de Boulogne*), was permitted to set up looms and install workers in the spacious rooms of the castle at Mantes.[86] Many received advances of money, without interest, to help them provide tools, machinery, and raw materials.[87] In 1606 two merchants of Rouen, Jean Wolff and Antoine Lambert, were promised 150,000 *livres* by the council of state out of the proceeds of the sale of lands from the royal domain in Normandy. They planned to manufacture *toille de Hollande* on a grand scale in a large building. The money was to help them in installing 150 looms. They were to keep 7,500 *livres* and to pay back the rest without interest within ten years.[88] In this way, Henri IV and his ministers earmarked several hundred thousand *livres* out of various royal taxes and other revenue from the provinces, to develop the manufacture of fine cloth and crystal glass within the realm.

Several of the new glass works, established with the help of royal privileges, were successfully carried on for a generation or more, although the craftsmen never succeeded in fashioning goblets, decanters, and vases of quite the transparency or the elegance of design that had made the

85 Cf. Hauser, *Les débuts du capitalisme*, pp. 123–4.

86 Archives Nationales, E24C, f. 340.

87 E.g., *ibid.*, E14A, f. 308; E16B, f. 160; E20A, f. 294v°.

88 *Ibid.*, E14A, ff. 65, 367.

finest Italian crystal glasses such perfect works of art.[89]
The privileged textile factories were generally less successful than the glass shops. Some failed even before they had
begun to produce any cloth. Only one or two, out of a score
or more, survived for more than a few years.[90] But the efforts of Henri IV and his ministers to set up royal textile
enterprises prepared the way for the great cloth manufactures of Louis XIV's reign, when Colbert applied similar
methods on a wider scale with much greater success.

A third form of government intervention was also associated with artistic craftsmanship and especially with the
fine arts. In this case the crown did not confine its support
to grants of privileges and capital. It established studios
and shops of its own. Ever since the end of the fifteenth
century, the French kings had employed groups of artisans
and artists to decorate and embellish the royal palaces with
beautiful hangings and works of art in stone and gold and
oil.[91] Francis I had induced Leonardo da Vinci and Ben-
venuto Cellini to work at his court.

Henri IV went much further in identifying the crown
with the artistic life of the nation. During his reign, and
especially during the reign of his successor, Louis XIII, the
court became the centre of an indigenous art and culture.
Court poets and writers, painters and musicians formulated
rules for French poetry and prose, for painting and music.
The great French classical tradition was being established.
The movement extended to the weaving of tapestry, to the
making of furniture, and to all the decorative arts. In the
medieval intellectual hierarchy, the artist who worked with
his hands to give form to matter had not been distinguished
from other craftsmen. Both were members of gilds with a
similar organization and similar rules. In the sixteenth
century, fine art was coming to be distinguished from ordinary manual work all over Europe. In France under Henri

[89] Cf. Nef, ''A Comparison of Industrial Growth,'' pp. 300–2.

[90] Cf. G. Fagniez, *L'économie sociale de la France sous Henri IV*, Paris,
1897, pp. 133–6, 140–1.

[91] Cf. Hauser, *Les débuts du capitalisme*, p. 117.

IV and Louis XIII, fine art was removed from the craft gilds and placed under the protection of the king and his councillors. At the beginning of the seventeenth century, there were 480 master craftsmen with their journeymen and apprentices in the employ of the court. The best painters and sculptors, clock makers, tapestry makers, and makers of mathematical instruments were installed in the great gallery of the Louvre.[92] Richelieu worked constantly to attach all national art to the court. The French crown was doing much to orient craftsmanship and industrial skill in the direction of the fine arts and the luxury trades, at a time when English artisans and technicians, less dependent than Frenchmen upon royal favors, were coming to concern themselves mainly with the invention of labor-saving machinery, with the substitution of mineral coal for firewood and charcoal, and with the production of material conveniences in large quantities.

Before the accession of Louis XIV, in 1643, the French crown had not only established a control through the gilds and municipal governments over the conditions of labor in old industries. It had staked out a claim to participate in the foundation and the development of all large workshops, factories, and considerable mines. It had also staked out a claim to participate in new ventures where large numbers of workpeople were employed for wages to labor in their own homes upon materials supplied from large warehouses. Little room was left in French industry for private initiative, except within the framework of the royal enactments and under the supervision of the royal officials. Artists, craftsmen, and inventors, together with industrial adventurers and wage hands, were all dependent for guidance and for success upon the king and his councillors.

The Saltpetre and Gunpowder Manufactures in England.

Against these solid accomplishments, the English crown had little to show on the eve of the civil war. That was not for want of trying. During the previous eighty years

[92] Hauser, *Débuts*, p. 117; *Ouvriers*, pp. 139–40.

or so, in Elizabeth's reign and especially in the reigns of James I and Charles I, the crown sought to obtain an interest in every new industry that developed within the realm, and to promote industrial monopolies in the hands of royal patentees. But such control as the crown secured over various industries was precarious and fleeting.

The nearest approach to direct government management was made in the armament industries. As in France, the king's title to a monopoly of the manufacture of saltpetre, gunpowder, and ordnance was based on the importance of munitions for the defense of the realm. The armament industries were organized under royal protection much later in England than in France,[93] and the English monarchs never found the administrative officers needed to bring them as completely under the control of the state as was done in France. It was not until the beginning of Elizabeth's reign, or just before it,[94] more than a hundred years after Charles VII and his councillors had taken the making of saltpetre and gunpowder into their own hands, that the gunpowder manufacture became important in England. According to an account written in 1630, the queen put the industry into the hands of Dutchmen and paid one of them £500 to teach two of her subjects to make saltpetre. Not many years afterward, the first patent for the sole making of saltpetre and gunpowder was granted to George Evelyn (1530–1603), grandfather of the famous diarist, and to his son John.[95] Evelyn belonged to a family of Norman origin that had settled in Shropshire and had later moved to Mid-

[93] In addition to the manufacture of saltpetre and gunpowder, which are treated in the text, the building of men-of-war and the casting of iron ordnance were done for the crown by contractors under the protection of royal officers (cf. Stowe MSS., 146; *Acts of the Privy Council*, 1547–50, pp. 77, 94, 165, 214, 234; State Papers Domestic, Eliz., vol. ccxxvii, no. 7; *Calendar of State Papers Domestic*, 1619–23, pp. 129, 230, 352, 487; *Hist. MSS. Com., Report on the MSS. of Earl Cowper*, vol. i, p. 126).

[94] Cf. *Victoria County History, Surrey*, vol. ii, p. 246.

[95] State Papers Domestic, Charles I, vol. clxxx, no. 10. There is some uncertainty as to the date of the first gunpowder patent granted to the Evelyns. From the accounts in the State Papers, it seems that the grant was made not earlier than 1559 and not later than 1568 (cf. *Calendar of State Papers Domestic*, 1601–3, p. 276).

dlesex. The exclusive privileges that he received for making gunpowder helped him to provide for his large family of sixteen sons and eight daughters. For more than half a century, until 1635, the royal gunpowder monopoly remained in the hands of his wealthy descendants,[96] though they sometimes shared it with city merchants like Richard Harding, who was included with two of George Evelyn's sons, John and Robert, in a patent of 1604.[97] The Evelyns had their powder mills at Long Ditton, in Surrey, and at other places south of London. Harding's powder plant was in a small village to the west of London, and he also owned a saltpetre house a little nearer to the city, at Hounslow.[98]

In 1588 the threat of the Spanish Armada put the English people and their rulers on the alert against a blockade and even an invasion. It brought home to them the importance of finding enough domestic saltpetre to make the nation independent of foreign supplies of both saltpetre and gunpowder. The queen's ministers granted royal commissions to a number of persons for the manufacture of saltpetre in the various counties of England and Wales.[99] The commissioners were authorized to ransack private buildings, barns, outhouses, stables, and birdhouses for the earth they needed in their manufacture. They had to send their petre to London for use at the powder mills of the Evelyns.

After the accession of James I, in 1603, some of the saltpetre men informed him that they had difficulties in carrying out their commissions because the control of ammunition was not in the hands of a person of high rank.[100] In response to this complaint, both the saltpetre commissioners and the gunpowder patentees were placed, in 1607, under the direction of the Earl of Worcester, the famous courtier who inherited a great place as patron of poetry and music from his father, a friend of Spenser. He retained this au-

96 *Ibid.*, 1634–5, p. 561.
97 State Papers Domestic, James I, vol. ix, no. 68.
98 Star Chamber Proceedings, 8/128/18 and 19.
99 Landsdowne MSS., 58, no. 63; Harleian MSS., 1926, no. 118.
100 State Papers Domestic, Charles I, vol. clxxx, no. 10.

thority until 1619 or 1620,[101] when it was transferred to three of King James' most trusted councillors, Buckingham, then lord admiral, Lord Carew, the master of the ordnance, and Sir Lionel Cranfield, then master of the court of wards,[102] upon whose business knowledge the king leaned heavily in all matters of economic policy. Like their predecessor, they issued royal commissions to saltpetre makers and entered into contracts with them for supplies of saltpetre and with the Evelyns for supplies of powder. The saltpetre commissioners were bound to deliver specified quantities of saltpetre to the gunpowder patentees, who contracted, in their turn, to buy the petre and sell a specified quantity of powder at fixed rates. The commissioners were bound to sell all their petre to the gunpowder patentees and the patentees were bound to sell all their powder to the king. If the king received more than he needed for his supplies of ammunition, he could sell the overplus for his own profit.[103]

Authorized by letters patent and proclamations but not by statutes, the saltpetre and gunpowder monopoly began to arouse much opposition in the house of commons and among the common-law judges at the beginning of the seventeenth century, when the commons took their first strong stand against monopolies in Queen Elizabeth's last parliament. Many of the complaints behind this opposition came from landlords and tenants, whose privacy had been invaded by the saltpetre commissioners in their search for earth. As Cecil admitted in speaking for the queen in parliament, the new patent dug "in everyman's house".[104]

[101] *Calendar of State Papers Domestic,* 1603–10, p. 356; State Papers Domestic, James I, Sign Manuel, 6/10; *Acts of the Privy Council,* 1618–19, pp. 247–8; F. C. Dietz, *English Public Finance, 1558–1641,* New York, 1932, p. 172.

[102] *Calendar of State Papers Domestic,* 1619–23, pp. 179, 216. When the commission was renewed in 1624, Cranfield was not included (*ibid.,* 1623–5, p. 300).

[103] Cf. State Papers Domestic, Eliz., vol. ccxxvii, no. 4; James I, vol. cxx, no. 102; Charles I, vol. clxxx, no. 10. If the powder makers were not paid by the crown within a specified time, they were at liberty to sell powder in the market.

[104] E. Lipson, *The Economic History of England,* London, vol. iii, 1931, p. 358.

What seemed worse to a nation of bird lovers, it dug in men's pigeon and dove houses, "the cheefest norses of saltpeter of this kingdome". To meet this objection, the Evelyns promised, in 1604, when they held the saltpetre as well as the gunpowder patent, not to allow the commissioners to dig for more than half an hour a day in any pigeon house, and to have them replace all eggs and pigeons that were lost.[105] Even if the commissioners had fulfilled these promises and had reconciled property holders to their expeditions by considerate treatment, opposition to the patent would have continued. It also came from another quarter, from the increasing number of town traders and landed gentlemen with money to invest in the new industries, the same persons who were becoming lax about complying with royal industrial legislation. They objected to all industrial monopolies as trenching upon the liberty and the property of the subject, whose rights, they claimed, were guaranteed by the fundamental law of the country.[106]

In answering this opposition, privy councillors generally took the line that the crown had regalian rights to saltpetre, the principal material used in making gunpowder. In a document written shortly before the death of Queen Elizabeth, and approved by Sir Thomas Fleming, the solicitor-general, and by Francis Bacon, whose power as her majesty's counsel was growing, it was pointed out that the most recent patent for the sole making of saltpetre and gunpowder had been drafted by the attorney-general himself, Sir Edward Coke, who had the confidence of the house of commons as a conscientious defender of the liberties of the subject. The patent was no monopoly, the authors of this document argued, because the making of saltpetre and gunpowder properly belonged to the crown and should not be undertaken without the queen's grant. The patent was "maintainable not only in policy for the preservation of the State, but also in equity, and by the common laws of the land".[107] It was doubtless on these grounds that a clause

105 State Papers Domestic, James I, vol. ix, no. 68.
106 See below, pp. 152-3.
107 *Calendar of State Papers Domestic*, 1601-3, p. 276.

exempting the manufacture of munitions was inserted in the famous statute of 1624 which declared monopolies illegal.[108]

Opposition to the patent was by no means silenced by these arguments. In 1603 many persons barred the way of the saltpetre men to their houses, claiming that the queen's death had cancelled the patent.[109] With the accession of Charles I, in 1625, new objections were urged against it. Even among the king's councillors, there were some who doubted whether the ammunition business was managed in the most efficient way by the monopoly they had been maintaining, whether the grant of exclusive privileges to the Evelyns and others produced the maximum quantity of powder that the natural resources of the country could be made to yield. While Elizabeth and James I had managed to steer clear of serious wars with foreign powers, so that they did not require nearly as much gunpowder as continental princes, troubles with France and Spain were brewing when King James died. These troubles brought on a series of naval engagements on the high seas and in foreign ports during the five years that followed. Larger supplies of powder were urgently needed by the navy. The monopolists were unable to deliver them.[110] Try as they would, the saltpetre commissioners in the various counties never managed to supply much more than three-fourths of the petre they were under contract to furnish John Evelyn,[111] an uncle of the diarist. Evelyn asked to be allowed to buy foreign saltpetre to make up for the deficiency, but few privy councillors wanted to grant him that right. Some were not sure it was desirable to have the royal commis-

[108] 21 Jac. I, cap. 3, para. x.

[109] State Papers Domestic, James I, vol. i, no. 64.

[110] *Calendar of State Papers Domestic*, 1627–8, p. 368; *Hist. MSS. Com., Report on the Lonsdale MSS.*, p. 45.

[111] State Papers Domestic, Charles I, vol. xxix, no. 40. Professor W. R. Scott says one-third (*The Constitution and Finance of English, Scottish and Irish Joint Stock Companies to 1720*, Cambridge, 1910, vol. ii, p. 472), but that would seem to be an understatement. For the deliveries of saltpetre in the years immediately preceding the civil war, see *Calendar of State Papers Domestic*, 1637–8, p. 242; 1640–1, pp. 240, 568.

sioners send all their saltpetre to Evelyn, instead of having it manufactured into gunpowder near where it was made,[112] as was done in France. Small mills making powder illegally, in defiance of the monopoly, had been multiplying in the west of England. In 1625 the privy council considered the advisability of breaking the contract with Evelyn and throwing the manufacture open to private enterprise.[113]

In the same year a resolution of the twelve judges of England, the greatest authorities on the common law, denied that the crown's interest in saltpetre found in the lands of subjects was comparable with its interest in gold and silver. The king could not dig for saltpetre earth; he had only the right to purvey it. He could not delegate this right of purveyance, but must employ his own agents. They might enter the buildings of a subject in search of earth, but only if they gave no annoyance and did no damage to property. There was nothing in the king's title to hinder private landlords or their tenants, without any royal commission, from making saltpetre on their own account from the materials in their buildings.[114] It is not clear whether the judges regarded the saltpetre commissioners as agents of the king. In any case their resolution struck a blow at the monopoly which had been upheld by parliament the year before.

Many new schemes for providing saltpetre and gunpowder were brought before the privy council during Charles I's reign. One was to have the municipal governments at Reading, Oxford, and other selected towns raise a stock to build and maintain saltpetre houses of their own, as was often done by municipal governments in France.[115] Another was to have every family in a thousand villages throughout the land prepare saltpetre on its own account for the king's service, under the supervision of the parish

112 *Ibid.*, 1625-6, p. 490.
113 State Papers Domestic, Charles I, vol. xi, nos. 24, 27.
114 Sloane MSS., 1039, f. 93.
115 State Papers Domestic, Charles I, vol. lxxiv, no. 45; *Calendar of State Papers Domestic*, 1627-8, p. 377.

clergy.[116] Nothing came of these schemes. Instead the privy council tried to preserve the old system, by maintaining the king's gunpowder contract with Evelyn and the royal commissions for making saltpetre for the service of his mills. But the monopoly was made less rigid than it had been. Evelyn could manufacture gunpowder only with the petre supplied by the royal commissioners, and the commissioners no longer held the exclusive right to make petre. Foreign saltpetre, and domestic saltpetre supplied by persons without a commission, could henceforth be made into gunpowder by anyone.[117] By 1627 the East India Company was allowed to manufacture powder from the saltpetre which it imported.[118] With the consent of the privy council another powder mill was set up at Bristol outside the patent.[119]

At the time of Charles I's accession, Lord Carew, who had had chief charge of the ammunition business during the last years of his father's reign, had predicted that if the East India Company were granted the right to make powder, it would "open a flood gate".[120] His prediction was coming true. The whole system of government control over the manufacture was collapsing.[121] John Evelyn complained that there was no sale for his gunpowder, because of the enterprise established by the East India Company.[122] In 1636 the king attempted to revive the monopoly. It was taken out of the hands of the Evelyns and entrusted to two new patentees, one of whom built mills at Chilworth, in Surrey, with the help of capital advanced out of the royal revenue.[123] The lords of the admiralty ordered the mayor

[116] State Papers Domestic, Charles I, clxxx, no. 4. For other schemes see Scott, *op. cit.*, vol. ii, p. 472; *Calendar of State Papers Domestic*, 1627–8, p. 2; 1634–5, p. 29.

[117] State Papers Domestic, Charles I, vol. civ, no. 71; vol. cxlii, no. 57.

[118] *Calendar of State Papers Domestic*, 1627–8, p. 492.

[119] State Papers Domestic, Charles I, vol. cclxv, no. 91.

[120] *Calendar of State Papers Domestic*, 1623–5, p. 489.

[121] Cf. *ibid.*, 1627–8, p. 493; 1628–9, p. 118; State Papers Domestic, Charles I, vol. ccxc, no. 42.

[122] *Calendar of State Papers Domestic*, 1627–8, p. 492.

[123] *Ibid.*, 1636–7, p. 148; 1639–40, p. 512; Privy Council Register, vol. xlvi, p. 368.

of Bristol to suppress the powder mills in that town.[124]   But these efforts to restore the monopoly ended in failure.   In 1641 parliament threw the manufacture open to everyone, as had been repeatedly proposed.   In 1656 parliament also took away the saltpetermen's right of forcible entry into private property in search of saltpetre.[125]

The monopoly which the English parliament rejected differed in important respects from the one which the French kings established and successfully maintained.   The manufacture of both saltpetre and gunpowder was left more under private management in England than in France. The royal administration entered the business directly only when the exchequer paid the gunpowder patentees for their deliveries of gunpowder at the Tower of London, where it was stored for the king's service,[126] and on the rare occasions when the king advanced money to help them in building their powder mills.   When a saltpetre commissioner needed capital to carry on his business he could seldom turn, as the French saltpetre masters so frequently turned, to the local governing officials for advances of money or loans of buildings and equipment.[127]   When he had saltpetre to deliver, there was no royal storehouse in the county to take it off his hands as in France.   He was left much more on his own resources than most French makers.

At the end of the sixteenth century, Richard Heaton, a commissioner in the North Riding of Yorkshire, became dependent for capital and for the transportation of his saltpetre upon a private merchant of Hull, named William Richardson.   Heaton's saltpetre house was at Malton, about thirty miles northwest of Hull.[128]   His servants delivered the saltpetre in hogsheads and barrels to Richardson's warehouse in Hull, to be shipped to London at Heaton's risk for sale to Robert Evelyn.   An agent of Richardson's, living in the city, delivered the saltpetre to

[124] *Calendar of State Papers Domestic*, 1637–8, pp. 32, 150.

[125] Scott, *op. cit.*, vol. ii, p. 472.

[126] Cf. State Papers Domestic, James I, vol. cxx, no. 102.

[127] Cf. *ibid.*, Charles I, vol. ccclxxvi, no. 155.

[128] Star Chamber Proceedings, 8/173/27.

Evelyn and sent the money he received for it to Richardson. Before he paid any money to Heaton, Richardson reimbursed himself for the costs of carriage and for debts owed him by Heaton for cash he had advanced. After Richardson's death, his son had Heaton thrown into prison for debts contracted in the saltpetre business, which Heaton claimed he had repaid.[129]

By restricting the manufacture of gunpowder to the Evelyns and a few other persons, the English privy council fostered large-scale enterprise in the munitions industry, at a time when the French government promoted a multitude of small enterprises in gunpowder as well as in saltpetre making. The restrictive nature of the English gunpowder patent did not make it popular with the majority of wealthy merchants and improving landlords who were investing their money in the rising industries. The situation was similar to that created by the royal mill at Bridgwater or the coal surveyorship at Newcastle. Powerful subjects objected to having the royal authority made the special preserve of particular individuals.

In the French gunpowder-making industry, the king was fostering old forms of enterprise to which the country was accustomed. His intervention was unfavorable, on the whole, to the concentration of industrial capital. In the English gunpowder-making industry, the monarch was fostering new forms of enterprise, requiring a large amount of private capital. Many English merchants and gentlemen were becoming interested in large enterprises of this kind in other industries, but few of them wanted participation in such enterprises restricted to one or two or a few court favorites. In France a large number of public officials throughout the country took part in managing the manufacture of saltpetre and gunpowder. This emphasized the impersonal character of the monopoly. In England where the privy council had no such administrative machinery at its disposal, the king's officials were active in managing the ammunition business only at the Tower and

129 Exchequer Depositions by Commission, 6 James I, East. 10.

in the chambers at Westminster. The royal manufacture of gunpowder was identified chiefly with one rich private family. There was plenty of illicit powder manufacturing outside the royal contracts in both countries. But it did not occur to Frenchmen, as it occurred to Englishmen, to attack the king's legal authority to maintain a royal monopoly of gunpowder manufacturing and to give royal commissioners the right to ransack private property for saltpetre earth.

The difference between the reception accorded the royal monopolies in the two countries can be explained in at least two ways. England's isolation from European wars during the late sixteenth and early seventeenth centuries, together with the protection that her insular position afforded from the threat of invasion, made the supply of ammunition less vital than in France, where enemies might attack at any time across the Pyrenees or the Alps, or with still greater ease from the low-lying country to the northeast. The habits of obedience to the royal authority in France provide a still more important explanation for the success of the French gunpowder and saltpetre monopoly. In England such habits of obedience to the economic regulations of princes as had existed in the Middle Ages and even in Tudor times, were being uproooted in the seventeenth century, partly because of the rapid rise of rich merchants and improving landlords to positions of power in the state. The Stuart policy of bringing large-scale enterprise under the control of the king and the privy council conflicted more and more with the economic interests of these classes, at a time when their growing wealth and self-confidence gave them the political and the moral strength to resist.

The Ownership of Mines in England.

If the English monarchs had difficulty in keeping the making of gunpowder in their own hands, they were not likely to fare better in other industries less obviously important to the state. Unlike the French kings, they never managed to establish a general system of supervision over mining or even a right to a share in the produce of all mines.

In England, as in France, at the beginning of the sixteenth century, the position of the king with respect to the ownership of ores and minerals was still not fully defined. Like continental princes, the English sovereigns had successfully claimed the possession of all ores containing gold or silver. Unlike most continental princes, they had not been successful in claiming a royalty from other ores and minerals mined in the lands of their subjects, though it is by no means certain that they had renounced the claim. It was only in connection with the tin mines of Devon and Cornwall, where the prince of Wales as duke of Cornwall had special rights, that the crown had derived a revenue from base ores dug within the manors of private landlords. The king's revenue from certain mines of lead ore in Derbyshire and from mines of iron ore and coal in the Forest of Dean was collected because the seams ran under royal lands. While the English crown probably had almost as large a part as the French crown in the mining carried on within the country at the end of the Middle Ages, the king was in a weaker position in England than in France to extend his regalian rights to cover all ores and minerals.

During the hundred years following the Reformation, the position of the English monarch was weakened still further by various decisions at common law. The most important was one given by the court of exchequer in 1566, at about the time when the first great expansion began in England in the mining of copper and lead ore, and above all coal. The dispute arose between the crown and the earl of Northumberland over the ownership of a seam of copper ore, containing some silver, at Newlands in Cumberland, under land owned by the earl. Judgment was given for the queen. But the judges laid it down as a principle that the rights of the crown did not extend to any ores or minerals unless they contained gold or silver. This made it impossible for the crown to claim, as was being done in France, that all mines were mines royal. The trend of decisions in the law courts during the late sixteenth and seventeenth centuries limited the regalian rights of the crown still further, because it was held that a mine of base ore must contain a substantial quantity of silver in order to be a mine royal.[130]   Mines royal of lead were defined by the king in 1623 as those "the oare whereof upon Essaye and tryall yeeldeth after the rate of eight ounces of silver out of every hundred waight of oare and 60 lbs. in lead".[131]   It is doubtful whether common-law judges would have agreed that mines containing so small a percentage of silver could be worked only with the king's permission.   According to one view expressed at the time, "all lead ore in England and Wales has silver in it, although not to the proportion of a royal mine".[132]

As Nature would have it, there were almost no mines in England that contained a substantial quantity of precious metals.   More and more private landlords found themselves free, except in a few areas where the king held the land, to mine for lead ore.   Over iron ore and coal the crown was never able to claim regalian rights.   Coal and all base ores were the property of the lord under whose manor or lordship they were found.   He was free to lease his mines as he pleased, and the royalty was paid to him and not to the crown.   Most of the large mining enterprises, started under Elizabeth and her two Stuart successors, were collieries. So the crown was left with little interest in mining and with no share in the return from the chief mines, unless they happened to be dug in lands belonging to the monarch.   As Elizabeth and the first two Stuarts sold much land to meet their current expenses, the mineral property of the crown dwindled.

The crown was never able to establish a national administration for the mines, like that of the French king.   When the monarch had some order to give in connection with mining, the task of carrying it out was entrusted to the ordinary

130 Cf. Nef, *Rise of the British Coal Industry*, vol. i, pt. iii, *passim.*
131 State Papers Domestic, James I, vol. clii, no. 9.
132 *Ibid.*, vol. cxlv, no. 66.

royal officials, the justices of the peace and the sheriffs.[133] Even in royal manors and forests, where the king or queen like any other landlord owned the minerals and appointed special officials to deal with their mining lessees, these officials, like the justices of the peace and the sheriffs, were always local men who were frequently more mindful of the wishes of their rich neighbors with investments in the mines than of the interests of their royal masters.[134] The tendency in England during the hundred years from 1540 to 1640 was not, as in France, for the sovereign to extend his authority over mining and metallurgy. Under the influence of decisions in the common-law courts, and under the pinch of financial necessity, the royal authority contracted at a time when the rapid expansion in the output of copper, lead, iron, and especially coal gave the mining and metallurgical industries a much greater importance in England than in France.

The Making of Salt in England.

The attempts of the English monarchs to participate in the manufacture of salt began in Elizabeth's reign. Salt making had been of small importance in medieval England. Between 1540 and 1640 the output grew something like fivefold.[135] With French experience before their eyes, English statesmen looked hopefully at the salt-making industry as a source of revenue. They saw a possibility of obtaining a royalty on salt made from sea water, by claiming that the foreshore, land between low and high tide, belonged to the state. Before the Reformation, salt produced from the brine springs of the Midlands or from sea water along the coasts had been made for the most part by town craftsmen and peasants, who usually accomplished their task without any considerable capital, by warming the water in vessels made of lead and generally no bigger than a washwoman's tub. It occurred to some of Elizabeth's ministers that the introduc-

[133] See, e.g., State Papers Domestic, James I, vol. clii, no. 9.
[134] Cf. Nef, *Rise of the British Coal Industry*, vol. i, p. 145.
[135] Nef, ''A Comparison of Industrial Growth,'' p. 297.

tion for the manufacture of salt from sea water of large iron pans, twenty feet and more across and heated by great furnaces, might serve as an excuse for imposing a tax on salt. The new works resembled those at Salins in Franche-Comté and at some places in Germany, where salt was generally made from brine springs. There the governing princes held shares in the enterprises, such as the queen's advisers apparently hoped to secure for her. Plans were made in 1563 and 1564, by William Cecil and other ministers of the crown, to bring in foreign workmen and advance capital for starting an enterprise with branches at Southampton, Dover, and along the coasts of Essex and Northumberland. By letters patent of 1564 the crown attempted to establish a national monopoly of the sale of salt from sea water. "The patent was to be the basis of an English gabelle."[136]

Nothing came of the project. The plant was set up, contracts were entered into with traders for the sale and delivery of the product, and the end of it all in three or four years' time was failure. The iron pans in Northumberland were rusting away unused five years after they had been installed.[137]

In the three decades following the collapse of this salt patent, private capitalists entered the industry, and a number of successful enterprises on a large scale were started, especially at the mouth of the Tyne and in Scotland. The claim of the crown to regalian rights in salt marshes along the coasts fared little better in the common-law courts than its claim to the ownership of base ores. In only three cases before 1640 was the sovereign able to establish this claim.[138] Neither James I nor Charles I found in the expanding salt industry a substantial resource. They could do little more about the *gabelle* than envy the French king his right to it, and the mounting returns that it brought into the French treasury.

136 Hughes, *op. cit.*, p. 32.

137 Cf. *ibid.*, pp. 31–5 and also Mr. Hughes' article, "The English Monopoly of Salt in the Years 1563–71," *English Historical Review*, XL (1925), pp. 334–50.

138 Hughes, *op. cit.*, p. 43.

The New Manufactures in England.

As we have seen, the introduction of new manufacturing processes and new branches of industry in France gave the French kings an opportunity to bring artists, master craftsmen, and wage-workers under royal protection. In England, the late sixteenth and early seventeenth centuries were a much more fertile period than in France for the introduction of labor-saving machinery, furnaces with strong blasts, and powerful engines for raising water from mines. More new branches of heavy industry were started. The people had to adjust themselves to the substitution of smoky coal fuel for wood and charcoal in their hearths and kitchen stoves, as well as in many of the kilns, forges, and furnaces of artisans and manufacturers. The new fuel stained their linen and increased their laundry bills. Many thought it gave them colds in the head and still more dreadful diseases. But they could not prevent coal from creeping into their lives, along with the technical improvements of the age, in spite of the protests of their wives, who clamored for country houses to take them out of reach of the stinking seacoal smell.

It was only in the luxury and artistic industries that the period was less fertile in new developments in England than in France. The age of Elizabeth and the first two Stuarts gave the world some of its most beautiful poetry and drama, a large portion of the finest prose works ever written in English, and the loveliest English songs. But it was a barren age for painting and sculpture and for all the decorative arts. The monarchs and the courtiers who encouraged the poets and the musicians by their patronage, did not follow the example of the French kings by fostering a national art that would bear the stamp of the royal arms in its conception and its spirit. They did not follow the example of Henri IV and Louis XIII in establishing royal studios and shops and in helping private persons to introduce fine glass blowing and beautiful weaving.

When it came to the heavy industries, the English monarchs were no less eager than the French to participate.

The difficulties were that they had not the capital, nor the authority, nor the officers needed to carry through a program of state enterprise embracing all the new branches of manufacturing. In spite of the patents which they granted for inventions, nearly all the successful inventions were made by men who got no protection from patents. In spite of their attempts to grant monopoly privileges for manufacturing, private persons continually challenged their right to limit enterprise to a particular individual or group of individuals.

Royal support was of much less value to the adventurers in occupations pursued primarily for private profit than to the artists and master craftsmen in occupations pursued primarily for the elegance and beauty of the objects fashioned in the workshops. The security of a small, sophisticated market of wealthy patrons, such as the court provided, combined with rules of good workmanship and true aesthetic principles, which the French kings could do much to foster if not to formulate, were the matters of principal importance to the artists and craftsmen engaged in the decorative arts and the luxury trades. Wide markets and efficient machinery, which the English kings could do little to provide, and low wage rates, which the privy council often instructed the justices of the peace to raise, were the matters of principal importance to the adventurers in heavy industries. So state participation in the new manufactures was bound to be less welcome in England than in France. The intervention of the crown became more and more unpopular among those groups of rich merchants and improving landlords who were acquiring large stakes in the industrial life of the country. Toward the end of the sixteenth century their opposition began to be voiced frequently in the house of commons and in the common-law courts. During the next four decades it grew so strong that it fanned the flames which produced the civil war.

At the beginning of Elizabeth's reign the crown embarked on a policy of granting letters patent to individuals or groups, giving them exclusive privileges in connection with one or another of the expanding industries. Sometimes these patents gave the sponsor of some invention the exclusive privilege to use it for a limited term of years.[139] Neither the house of commons nor the common-law judges ever took exception to patents of that kind. Occasionally, as in the case of Cecil's salt patent, the grant was intended to create a national monopoly of some manufacture in the hands of the patentees. The fate of these attempted monopolies was usually the same as that of the salt patent. The patentees failed to make good their promises. If they did not give up the work altogether, as the salt patentees did, they were soon faced with a number of competitors and obliged to abandon the attempt to maintain their exclusive privileges. As a result partly of these failures and partly of the view taken by the common-law judges that general monopolies were illegal, statesmen became more wary in their patent policy after the middle of Elizabeth's reign than they had been before. During the last two decades of the sixteenth century the privy council seldom supported general industrial monopolies. While a good many new industrial patents were granted, the rights of the patentees were usually limited either to the use of some new manufacturing process, not hitherto employed in England, or to particular places within the kingdom.

There was always a temptation for the queen's councillors to yield to appeals from her favorites, and to extend the scope of a patent that had been legitimate when it was granted, until it became in the eyes of the house or the common-law courts an abusive monopoly. That is what happened in the case of the patent issued to John Spilman, the naturalized German who had become the queen's jeweler. In 1588 he was granted the exclusive right to make white writing paper. His monopoly could be defended on the ground that this was a new process, for no such writing paper was apparently made in England at the time. It is doubtful whether Spilman himself succeeded in making it.

[139] W. H. Price, *The English Patents of Monopoly*, Cambridge (Mass.), 1906, pp. 7–8.

But the protection afforded by his patent helped him to maintain at Guildford, near London, his large mills for the manufacture of a rougher paper. In 1597 the queen gave him a new patent for the manufacture of paper of every description. According to the terms of this patent, no other person in the kingdom had a right to start a paper mill without Spilman's permission.[140] Competitors were already fairly numerous before the queen's death in 1603, and, after a few unsuccessful attempts to enforce his monopoly, Spilman contented himself with such a share of the expanding market for paper as the efficiency of his machinery, the skill of his workmen, and the situation of his mills enabled him to command.[141]

Even more limited patents than Spilman's were hard to maintain, partly because of the attitude of the common-law courts, but more especially because of the opposition of the justices of the peace—the very persons who were expected to enforce them! These officials showed no more sympathy for the patent policy of the crown than for its policy of industrial regulation. In 1588 the justices in Yorkshire refused to enforce a new salt patent, granted in 1585, and designed to monopolize the supply of one brand of salt in the three ports of Boston, King's Lynn, and Hull. It was discovered by the privy council that among the chief persons who defied the monopoly was one of the justices, Nicholas Hare. He had "presumed to impose himself against the authority of Her Majestie's . . . prerogative" and had brought four shiploads of contraband Scottish salt to King's Lynn to sell for his own profit.[142]

With the multiplication of private ventures in many industries during the phenomenally rapid expansion of mining and manufacturing that began about 1575, the gentry and the merchants became more and more disturbed by the

140 R. H. Clapperton, *Paper,* Oxford, 1934, p. 112; *Calendar of State Papers Domestic,* 1595-7, p. 450; Nef, ''A Comparison of Industrial Growth,'' pp. 658–9.

141 Cf. Clapperton, *op. cit.,* pp. 112–5; *Calendar of State Papers Domestic,* 1598–1601, p. 505; 1601–3, pp. 43–4.

142 Hughes, *op. cit.,* pp. 62–3.

royal patent policy. They began to see in the crown an economic rival. The growing resentment felt among these classes toward monopolies found expression in 1601, in Elizabeth's last parliament, when the commons protested so strongly that the queen summoned them to Whitehall, where she made a famous and most artful speech professing her desire to redress their grievances. In 1603, the year of her death, the famous decision was given in the court of queen's bench, which declared a monopoly of the making of playing cards a dangerous innovation contrary to common law. The judges drew a line between legitimate and illegitimate patents of monopoly, which has been the basis of the common law ever since. Patents might legally be granted "when any man by his own charge, or by his own wit or invention doth bring any new trade into the realm, or any engine tending to the furtherance of a new trade that never was used before; and that for the good of the realm". Such patents were to last only for a reasonable term of years, until Englishmen had time to learn the new methods.[143]

In spite of this decision, in what has come to be called the case of monopolies, James I was less cautious than his predecessor in his attempts to bring industry under royal control. He even revived the policy of the early part of Elizabeth's reign and attempted to set up general monopolies in some industries, notably in the production of the alum needed by the textile manufacturers to dye their cloth and in the making of glass.

The alum plant in Yorkshire was the nearest thing in England in James I's reign to the royal manufactures of the French kings. Patents for alum making were not new. Queen Elizabeth had entered into agreements with various adventurers, granting them exclusive rights to manufacture alum and also copperas, another important dye. Sometimes the adventurers received advances of capital. Under the terms of the agreements, the crown was generally en-

[143] Darcy v. Allen. See the summary of the case in Price, *op. cit.*, pp. 23–4. Cf. Heckscher, *op. cit.*, vol. i, p. 283.

titled to a portion of the output, and was permitted to buy the remainder at a lower price than that paid for foreign alum.[144] Some alum was being manufactured, at the time of the queen's death, in Dorset and the Isle of Wight, and probably in the North Riding of Yorkshire [145] and elsewhere. James I and his ministers were persuaded by a syndicate of four prominent adventurers, represented at court by Lord Sheffield, president of the council of the north, to organize the manufacture near the Yorkshire coast as a great royal monopoly.[146] In January, 1607, the adventurers were granted a patent for thirty-one years.[147] With the help of money lent by several London merchants, they brought skilled workmen from Germany and Italy to help build and equip a number of alum houses, at a cost of tens of thousands of pounds. The adventurers had little financial success and they abandoned their direct interest in the enterprise sometime between 1609 and 1613, heavily in debt.[148]

In 1613 the king took the works into his own hands and confided their management to three merchants who had replaced the original contractors. An attempt was made to establish an enterprise apparently modeled on that near Rome, where alum making had been taken into the hands of the pope as early as 1462. During the six years from 1612 to 1617 the crown advanced nearly £70,000 toward the maintenance of the works and the payment of the creditors [149] who had put up much of the money for the original

[144] State Papers Domestic, Eliz., vol. cx, no. 40 (William Kendall's monopoly); Exchequer Special Commission, no. 710 (Cornelius de Vos' patent assigned to the Earl of Mountjoy); State Papers Domestic, Eliz., vol. xl, no. 50; vol. lxxxv, no. 45; vol. ccxliv, no. 109; vol. ccl, no. 51 (Lord Mountjoy's monopoly, later purchased by the Earl of Huntington).

[145] North Riding Quarter Sessions, vol. ii, p. 22 note; vol. iv, p. 71 note.

[146] Price, op. cit., p. 83.

[147] Ibid. Cf. Hist. MSS. Com., Report on the MSS. of the Earl Cowper, vol. i, p. 84.

[148] Price, op. cit., pp. 83–5. Cf. Calendar of State Papers Domestic, 1603–10, p. 600.

[149] F. C. Dietz, ''The Receipts and Issues of the Exchequer during the reigns of James I and Charles I,'' Smith College Studies in History, vol. xiii, no. 4 (1928), pp. 160–1. Cf. State Papers Domestic, James I, vol. lxxv, no. 67.

plant, and who were said to number 180.[150] A small part of
this sum, something like £3,000, was spent on the manufacture of alum in the Isle of Purbeck in Dorset, where the
houses were treated as an adjunct to the royal manufacture
in the north.[151] The three contractors who represented the
king leased out the various houses in the north to experts in
the manufacture, and these experts undertook to make alum
at a stipulated price, much as Evelyn agreed to make gunpowder for the royal stores. The contractors then sold the
alum for the king's profit.

This arrangement was short-lived and unsuccessful.
In 1615 the works were again farmed out to a group of
London merchants.[152] It was not until 1621 that they began
to yield the crown a return. In spite of the great depression in the cloth-making industry, they brought £19,841 into
the exchequer between 1621 and 1625, the year James I
died.[153] It was not until after 1630, when the Yorkshire
works were farmed out to a new patentee, that the crown
got back all the money it had advanced between 1612 and
1617.[154]

In the time of James I alum stones were found in several manors in different parts of England. The king does
not appear to have claimed regalian rights to these stones,
but his officers did try to prevent all manufacture of alum
outside the patent. In 1612, in the court of exchequer, the
crown asked for an injunction to stop Sir Richard Houghton
from making alum in his manor of Houghton in Lancashire,
where the necessary stones had been found. This court had
declared half a century before, in the case of mines,[155] that
only minerals containing gold and silver belonged to the
crown. In Houghton's defense, it was suggested that he
was free to exploit his mineral wealth as he saw fit, because

[150] Price, *op. cit.*, p. 89.

[151] Exchequer Depositions by Commission, 22 James I, Hilary 29.

[152] Cf. Star Chamber Proceedings, James I, 8/158/3.

[153] Dietz, *op. cit.*, pp. 142–3.

[154] *Ibid.*, pp. 146, 160–1. A good general account of the enterprise under
James I is in Price, *op. cit.*, pp. 83–95.

[155] See above, p. 99.

the manor contained no "Mines Royall or prerogative of gold or silver".[156]   But he seems to have given up his manufacture, possibly because he became interested shortly afterward in the sale of alum from the royal works.[157]   As the making of alum was by no means novel, it is difficult to understand on what grounds the crown was able to enforce the patent and to get it exempted from the statute against monopolies passed by parliament in 1624.[158]

The grounds for exempting the glass-making patent are clearer.   That patent was granted by the crown in 1615, for an annual rent of £1,000, to a group of nine adventurers, all of whom were soon bought out by Sir Robert Mansell, the courtier and admiral.[159]   Mansell undertook to pay each of the nine original patentees an annual rent of £200.[160]   Unlike the holders of the alum monopoly, he received no advances of money from the crown, nor did the king ever attempt to set up a direct control over the glass manufacture as he did over the alum manufacture.   The king never appointed royal officials to manage the glass works or the sale of glass.   All profits from the venture went to Mansell.

Glass making was even less novel than alum making. Glass had been blown in England for many generations. Improved methods had been introduced by immigrants from Lorraine, the Low Countries, France, and Italy at the beginning of Elizabeth's reign, fifty years before Mansell had his patent.[161]   The excuse for granting the new patent was the important discovery, some years before 1615, of a method of making glass with coal instead of wood fuel.[162]

156 Exchequer Depositions by Commission, 10 James I, East. 8.

157 *Hist. MSS. Com., Report on the MSS. of the Earl Cowper,* vol. i, p. 84.

158 21 Jac. I, cap. 3, para. xi.

159 Price, *op. cit.,* pp. 72–3; *Calendar of State Papers Domestic,* 1619–23, p. 176; *Acts of the Privy Council,* 1615–16, pp. 469–73.

160 *Calendar of State Papers Domestic,* 1619–23, p. 491.

161 For some of the documents, see State Papers Domestic, Eliz., vol. xlii, nos. 42, 43, 45, 46, 56. Cf. A. Hartshorne, *Old English Glasses,* London, 1897, pp. 157, 191–2; Price, *op. cit.,* pp. 67–70; Nef, ''A Comparison of Industrial Growth,'' pp. 305–6.

162 Nef, ''The Progress of Technology and the Growth of Large Scale Industry, 1540–1640,'' p. 16.

While none of the patentees apparently had anything to do with the invention, the patent conferred the exclusive right to establish coal-burning furnaces. This limited monopoly was soon ingeniously converted into a general one. A royal proclamation of 1615 prohibited all glass making in England with wood fuel, in the interest of timber conservation, and forbade the importation of glass.[163] The holders of an earlier patent for manufacturing glass in Ireland with wood fuel had some of their cases seized by agents of Mansell when they reached Bristol. Before 1619 the furnaces built in Ireland with the capital of London merchants had failed.[164] Mansell set about to persuade the privy council to pull down all furnaces working without his license. In the summer of 1623 some glass-making houses in Dorset were destroyed by order of the council.[165] Although Mansell still had several competitors in England, and although he was not successful in preventing imports of glass from Scotland,[166] his patent left him with a legal claim to monopolize the English glass market.

How shall we account for James I's attempt to pursue such a vigorous policy with respect to industrial monopolies? It was apparently due partly to his Scottish origin, partly to the views of some of his advisers, and no doubt also partly to his general perverseness, which was as galling to some of his contemporaries as it has become amusing to historians. In Scotland a patent system had existed without challenge. There the king had participated in some of the chief enterprises, by advancing money, as was frequently done in France.[167] When it came to the precise terms of the English patents, a good deal hinged on the position taken by the attorney-general, who had charge of drafting them. If the office was held by a man who favored

[163] Price, *op. cit.*, pp. 72–3.

[164] Exchequer Depositions by Commission, 16 James I, East. 2.

[165] *Calendar of State Papers Domestic*, 1611–18, p. 601; Exchequer Depositions by Commission, 22 James I, East. 24.

[166] Cf. *Acts of the Privy Council*, 1621–1623, pp. 329–30.

[167] Hughes, *op. cit.*, p. 70.

common law like Sir Edward Coke, he was likely to be more mindful of the rights of the subject, particularly the subject who had an interest in private industrial ventures, than of the importance of the crown prerogative. Coke was attorney-general from 1593 to 1606. In June, 1607, a few months after the royal alum monoply in Yorkshire was established, Francis Bacon was made solicitor-general. He was promoted to attorney-general in 1613, shortly after the king took the alum enterprise into his own hands, and on the eve of the establishment of the glass monopoly. A fear was expressed at the time of his promotion that he might "prove a dangerous instrument of monarchy".[168] This was not surprising in view of his record on the monopoly question. He had opposed the agitation against monopolies in the parliament of 1601, and had insisted that the house of commons was encroaching upon the royal prerogative by attempting to limit and define the rights of the crown with respect to patents.[169]

As a result partly of the efforts made by James I and some of his advisers to increase the share of the crown in the expanding industries, the struggle over patents in the house of commons was renewed during the last years of his reign in a more acute form than ever before. The difficulty of maintaining government-controlled monopolies in connection with any industry was increased by the passage, in 1624, of the celebrated statute of monopolies. This made it illegal to grant exclusive rights for manufacturing except to protect inventors of new industrial processes for terms of fourteen years. The gunpowder-, the alum-, and the glass-making patents were the only important industrial monopolies exempted. It is probable that the house allowed the glass and alum patents to stand, after an agreement had been reached with the king's legal advisers that these would lapse when their terms ran out, and that no similar monopolies would be granted in other industries.

168 *Ibid.*, pp. 77–8.
169 Price, *op. cit.*, p. 21.

Industrial Monopolies under Charles I.

If such a promise was made, it was not kept by Charles I. As his struggle with the house over his constitutional prerogative became more serious, as religious issues grew sharper, the years of personal government began and the king attempted to govern without parliament. Such an attempt could succeed only if he had sufficient power to raise money, as Hobbes remarked, writing in the shadow of the constitutional struggle. In his desperate search for revenue, Charles turned hopefully to industry. The mines and heavy manufactures were producing something like six, seven, or eight times as large a volume of commodities as in the reign of Henry VIII, a hundred years before. For some decades crown lawyers, like Bacon, had been urging in pamphlets, petitions, and letters that the king's prerogative might legitimately be stretched to cover the control of trade and even the partial ownership of some of the principal industries.

The difficulties involved in putting such a conception of the prerogative into practice had become almost insuperable. In France the crown had participated successfully in large-scale enterprise before the field was occupied by private capitalists, and private capitalists had shown little disposition to compete with their royal master. But in England, before the accession of Charles I, private merchants or landlords, who owed nothing to royal support, were already deeply engaged in most heavy industries, either directly through investments in mines and manufacturing enterprises, or indirectly through their trade in the products. Some of them were members of the house of commons. Many were magistrates in London, in the chief provincial towns, and in the industrial shires.

Charles' advisers shied at adopting the bolder schemes presented to them for participating in mining and manufacturing. Some of these schemes aimed at nothing less than what we should now call the complete socialization of an industry and the elimination of some of the capitalist traders who were obtaining most of the profits. It would have been an extremely hazardous adventure to try to replace the private capitalists in established industries by contractors bound to serve the king, even if the crown had found the means to buy them out. Industrial monopolies were in discredit, not only because of the decisions and acts against them at common law and in parliament, but because the monopolies tolerated by the house in alum, glass, and gunpowder making were breaking down. The management of the enterprises was frequently bad, and competition from private ventures threatened their existence.[170] Complaints against the quality of the glass made under Mansell's patent were frequent. The tempers of some of the leading magistrates of London were rising at the prospect that new schemes of state interference might be adopted to the damage of their fortunes. Their attitude was coming to concern some of Charles' ministers. In 1628 Sir Francis Cottington, who was restored to the king's favor after the assassination of Buckingham and made a privy councillor, suggested that one of the schemes, designed to take the coal industry into the hands of the state, if put in practice, would cause a rebellion.[171]

The king's only hope of sharing extensively in the mounting profits from heavy industries seemed to rest upon his coming to an agreement with the powerful merchants and landlords who were already in control of some of them. The statute of monopolies had not been directed against corporations for the benefit of trade or companies of merchants. Section 9 specifically excluded them from molestation. Crown lawyers believed that the terms of this section might be stretched to cover industrial monopolies, if they were granted to a corporation of adventurers rather than to an individual.[172] Charles grasped at this straw. He and his advisers rejected the ambitious schemes for state control brought before the privy council, and adopted a

170 Cf. State Papers Domestic, Charles I, vol. ccclxxviii, no. 58.

171 Nef, *Rise of the British Coal Industry*, vol. ii, p. 276.

172 21 Jac. I, cap. 3; S. R. Gardiner, *History of England*, London, 1884, vol. viii, pp. 71-2.

more timid course than the sponsors of these schemes had advocated. The prospect of disaster held the king back from bold, forthright action, and, as is so often the case when some action is imperative, caution did not prevent the disaster.

After parliament had been dissolved in 1629, not to reassemble for nearly twelve years, the privy council set about to make deals with the large producers in one industry after another. They had partial success with the alum makers, whom they already controlled, and also with the soap makers. Beginning in 1630, when it was granted to a new patentee,[173] the alum patent brought considerable sums into the exchequer, amounting to about £126,000 during the eleven years ending in 1640.[174] In 1632 and again in 1637 the king made contracts with groups of soap makers. The first company consisted partly of Catholic friends of the lord treasurer, the Earl of Portland, who died a Catholic in 1635, and whose son, Sir Richard Weston, owned an important soap house in London.[175] This favoritism shown to Portland's friends caused much scandal. It aroused the anger of Archbishop Laud, who worked as a member of the privy council against the company. The second company, which had Laud's support and which agreed to buy out the first, was much less exclusive. It consisted of all the chief manufacturers of London. Along with the manufacturers of Bristol and Bridgwater, they were granted the sole right to make soap in England, though some small independent producers in York and other towns were allowed to continue their operations.[176] These arrangements with soap makers enabled the king to raise another £122,000 between 1634 and 1640.[177]

[173] *Calendar of State Papers Domestic,* 1629–31, p. 553.
[174] Dietz, *op. cit.,* pp. 146–7, 150.
[175] Exchequer K. R. Accounts, Misc., 634/16.
[176] Gardiner, *op. cit.,* vol. viii, pp. 72–7, 284; Price, *op. cit.,* pp. 119–23; State Papers Domestic, Charles I, vol. ccclxiii, no. 17; *Calendar of State Papers Domestic,* 1637–8, p. 142; 1638–9, p. 240; 1639–40, p. 602; Privy Council Register, Charles I, vol. x, p. 104; vol. xiv, pp. 28, 39, 91–2.
[177] Dietz, *op. cit.,* pp. 147, 150.

His financial advisers proposed to extend this system of participation to most of the important industries in the kingdom. The king entered into agreements with the principal salt manufacturers of the Tyne valley,[178] with the coal owners of Newcastle, and with the chief wholesale coal traders of the south of England.[179] Plans on foot during the winter of 1635–36 to establish a corporation of brick makers in London and the suburbs, were carried through in 1636. The corporation was to pay the king 6d. for every thousand bricks produced.[180] In each case, the crown granted a patent incorporating the capitalists who controlled the industry. It undertook to guarantee them a monopoly in supplying the realm, or at least the most important centres of population, for a period of fourteen years, the limit prescribed for patents of invention in the statute of 1624.[181] The king hoped to make the patents popular by bringing down prices, so the privy council got the patentees to promise to sell their commodities at or below rates stipulated in the agreements. The participants undertook to pay the crown many thousands of pounds annually for their privileges. If these schemes had all been successful, the king might have received a much larger revenue than he got from soap making and alum making, industries of smaller importance than salt making, coal mining, or the manufacture of bricks. The coal industry alone might have been made to yield something like £100,000 a year.[182] The king might have been able to meet the expenses of government without calling parliament.

It was a fundamental weakness of all these patents that, without gaining enthusiastic support from the participants, they aroused the hostility of the interests left out. In no case had the capitalists who joined in the agreements any

178 Hughes, *op. cit.*, pp. 88–115.

179 Nef, *op. cit.*, vol. ii, pp. 279–83.

180 *Calendar of State Papers Domestic*, 1639, p. 66; Gardiner, *op. cit.*, vol. viii, p. 283.

181 21 Jac. I, cap. 3, section vi.

182 Nef, ''Dominance of the Trader in the English Coal Industry,'' in *Journal of Economic and Business History*, vol. i, no. 3 (1929), p. 432.

vital reasons for maintaining an arrangement which did no more than support them in a position they had obtained without help from the state. The privileges offered were for the most part empty. They already had them. The king's chief motive was obvious to all but the most obtuse. It was revenue. Such a motive on the part of one party to the contract was not likely to temper the greed of the other. Unless the capitalists were able to increase their profits, the contracts were of no advantage to them. When the price-fixing clauses interfered with their profits, they did not hesitate to sell their products at rates above those permitted, if they could not find a way, as the brick makers did, of evading the spirit of their contracts by charging exorbitant prices for carriage.[183] Such evasions alienated the buyers, some of whom had been favorably disposed toward state participation in industry, because they thought it might spare them from high prices and short measure at the hands of unscrupulous private traders.[184] The king's new patent policy was left with few defenders in any quarter soon after it was launched.

The crown was in a less effective position to enforce these patents than it had been fifty or even twenty years earlier. Statute law, as well as common law, could now be cited against them. As the interests of judges, justices of the peace, and members of the house of commons in large-scale industry had increased, their dislike had grown for crown interference with the free play of economic forces. They became less and less disposed to help the king in any arrangement which enabled him to raise money independently of parliament. The coal, the salt, and the brick patents were not being enforced three years after they had been issued.[185] Unlike the alum and soap monopolies they brought little money to the exchequer.

[183] Gardiner, *op. cit.*, vol. viii, p. 283.

[184] Cf. Nef, ''Dominance of the Trader in the English Coal Industry,'' p. 433.

[185] For coal and salt, see Nef, *Rise of the British Coal Industry*, vol. ii, pp. 279–82, and Hughes, *loc. cit.;* for brick making, *Calendar of State Papers Domestic*, 1639, p. 116; State Papers Domestic, Charles I, ccccxxv, no. 31 (2).

Their collapse further discredited the system of industrial patents at the very time when opposition to the political and religious policies of the crown was becoming intense. When want of money forced the king to summon parliament in 1640, the house of commons put an end to nearly all industrial monopolies, including those exempted from the statute of 1624. The soap-makers' company retained their privileges, on the ground that, unlike most other monopolists, they did not engross the manufacture into a few hands.[186] But the glass and alum patents were condemned and abolished,[187] along with the gunpowder patent. All restrictions on the number of printing houses and presses were lifted.[188] The nucleus for a system of royal manufactures, such as the French kings had successfully established, was destroyed.

All that was left of the attempt made by the English monarchy to participate in industry was its authority to protect inventors by granting them patents for the discovery of new technological methods, with exclusive privileges for a limited period of fourteen years. The common-law judges and the members of parliament had already endorsed such patents. As the authority of common law and the power of the house of commons increased, the patent system was strengthened. In France, where the general control of industry by the state was so much greater than in England, no patent system like that of the English was established until late in the eighteenth century. The policy of granting inventors special protection, which had begun in France as in England about the middle of the sixteenth century,[189] was submerged in the general policy of making

[186] Price, *op. cit.*, pp. 125–8.

[187] *Ibid.*, pp. 78, 99.

[188] Cf. above, p. 30.

[189] Price's suggestion that the systematic use of patents for invention in France in Henri IV's reign may have been "in imitation of the English patent system" (*op. cit.*, p. 5), seems improbable. Apparently the first patent for an invention granted by the French crown preceded the first patent granted by the English crown (cf. Hauser, *Ouvriers du temps passé*, pp. 136–7; Price, *op. cit.*, p. 4).

all large industrial enterprises dependent upon royal privileges. In England the common-law judges, the justices of the peace, and the members of the house detached the patent system frőm the general policy of government participation in industry, with which it had little in common, and discarded what remained.

Why was the maintenance of the patent system the one industrial policy of the English monarchy welcomed by the majority of members of parliament, judges, and magistrates during the decades preceding the civil war? Their support was prompted partly by self-interest. The increasing industrial investments of the wealthy merchants and the improving landlords, represented in parliament, in the courts, and in the town governments, led them to welcome any invention designed to reduce costs of production and to increase profits. Some of them were in sore need of engines to drain their mines. A larger number, with interests in manufactures, found the costs of fuel mounting so rapidly, as the neighboring trees and shrubbery were cut down and grubbed up, that they were faced with failure unless means were found to make possible the burning of coal in place of charcoal, logs, and billets. Such industrial adventurers and their political representatives saw in the granting of patents a means of encouraging the search for the new inventions with which their prosperity was increasingly bound up.

Their support of the policy of granting patents to inventors will be imperfectly understood if it is regarded as prompted solely by self-interest. Some of the more scientifically-minded merchants and landed gentlemen were coming to believe that the encouragement of inventors was essential to material improvement, to the multiplication of commodities which would increase the comfort and which might improve the health of the nation. They saw in the patent policy a means of stimulating the technical ingenuity which according to English philosophers, Francis Bacon in particular, might create an earthly paradise. They were not persuaded that any of the other industrial policies contributed to prosperity. Such policies were better suited to France, where industrial progress consisted chiefly in improvements in the arts and crafts, than to England, where industrial progress consisted chiefly in the multiplication of material conveniences. They found their selfish interests and the new philosophy, with its emphasis on material improvement, leading them in the same direction. Both encouraged them to oppose the meddlesome interference of the king and the privy council with industry.

CHAPTER 4

FINANCIAL AND AGRARIAN POLICIES

Although industry was acquiring a greatly increased importance in the national economy of England in the late sixteenth and early seventeenth centuries, in all probability it still employed on the eve of the civil war a smaller number of persons than either commerce or agriculture. The financial and the agrarian policies of the monarchy aroused at least as much hostility as the industrial policies among the merchants and the improving landlords.[1] This hostility was partly the result of their interests in trade and farming, but it was also the result of their interests in mining and manufacturing. Both the financial and the agrarian policies of the English monarchy handicapped them indirectly in their efforts to develop new mines and manufactures. The opposition of the merchants and the gentry to these policies would have been less bitter than it was had there been, as in France, no very rapid growth of heavy industry between the Reformation and the civil war. Nor would the merchants and the gentry have been in as strong a position as they were to challenge the king's authority in financial and agrarian matters, if, as in France, their stake in large-scale industry had not greatly increased.

Financial Policy in Relation to Industry.

In the sixteenth and early seventeenth centuries, the king could not strengthen his authority if he continued to live on the resources to which he was entitled as the great-

[1] Professor R. H. Tawney treated this subject at length in a series of lectures, given at the University of Chicago in the spring quarter of 1939, on the economic background of the English revolutions. For an adequate understanding of the opposition to the financial and agrarian policies of the crown, we must await his forthcoming book.

est of feudal lords, or if he was dependent for further supplies of money upon a representative assembly capable of acting counter to his will. Greater financial resources were indispensable not only for waging war, but for carrying out any of the important domestic policies, including the industrial policies. The regulation of industry by the crown and the participation of the crown in large-scale enterprise might turn out to be profitable. But a substantial return could hardly be expected without a large outlay. The expenses of enforcing the industrial regulations and of controlling enterprises under royal tutelage were great, for it was necessary to pay for the services of a large corps of loyal civil servants concerned with industrial administration in the provinces as well as in the capital. Royal or privileged mines and manufactures could be established and maintained only if the king were prepared to advance large amounts of capital to provide buildings and equipment. Again, a program of social reform, like that attempted by the English crown under the early Stuarts, involved the assumption of responsibilities for the unemployed. In 1622, for example, the privy council decided to give 3*d*. a day to persons in several counties who had been thrown out of work by the great depression in the textile trades.[2]

During the hundred years from 1540 to 1640 the French kings succeeded in finding the additional revenue essential for carrying through a program of industrial regulation and control, and for strengthening royal absolutism. The English monarchs were blocked from doing so by the opposition of the house of commons and the taxpayers.

At the beginning of the sixteenth century the French king had considerable power to tax traders, peasants, and craftsmen. His power to exact forced loans was already great. The loans often bore no interest and the principal was not always repaid. With the French king's financial power possibly in his mind, the Emperor Maximilian remarked at this time that he himself was a king of kings,

2 *Calendar of State Papers Venetian,* 1621–3, pp. 249–50.

because no man felt bound to obey him. The king of Spain, he said, was a king of men, because though people reproached him they did his bidding. But the king of France was a king of beasts, because no man dared refuse him anything.[3] This comment on the abject character of human beings who render blind obedience to a sovereign contains a lesson for modern despots and supporters of despotism.

In Maximilian's time the French king's power to raise money was less impressive than it became in the seventeenth century, with the triumph of royal absolutism under Henri IV and Louis XIII. During their reigns, which lasted from 1589 to 1643, the French crown finally established a title that went unchallenged for more than a century afterwards, to raise the greater portion of its revenue by direct taxes on the wealth of the third estate, without the consent of their representatives. Most of the revenue came from the *taille* and the *gabelle*.

The *taille* was levied chiefly on the income or the real property of peasants, shopkeepers, and those craftsmen, traders, and entrepreneurs who were not exempted because of their participation in the royal manufactures. It was the nobles, the churchmen,, and the royal officials who escaped. As a permanent tax, collected every year, the *taille royale* had been established in 1439, somewhat later than the *gabelle*. Together with the *grande crue*, established in the reign of François I, and the *taillon*, established in the reign of his son, Henri II, the *taille* yielded a much larger return than the *gabelle*. Each year the king's council fixed the total amount which it was expected to bring in. This sum was then divided and subdivided among the various administrative divisions of the country, and finally among the persons subject to the tax in each parish. The return increased from some three million *livres* per annum, at the beginning of the sixteenth century,

[3] L. von Ranke, *Französische Geschichte*, 4th ed., Leipzig, 1876, vol. i, p. 87; cited by Richard Ehrenberg, *Capital and Finance in the Age of the Renaissance* (Eng. translation), London, 1928, p. 61.

to almost forty-two million *livres* during the five years, 1636 to 1640,[4] more than twice the revenue from the *gabelle* and the other taxes on salt at this time.[5] The *gabelle* fell heavily on the same persons who paid the *taille*. It was more in the nature of a direct than an indirect tax, because the consumer of salt was not at liberty to take the quantity he pleased.[6] As we have seen, the yield from the *gabelle* increased about fortyfold between the early sixteenth century and the death of Louis XIII in 1643.[7] Finally, the crown succeeded in increasing notably the yield of the indirect taxes (of which the principal were the *aides*) on the sale of various commodities, including wine, cider, beer, wheat and other necessities of life.[8] Like the *taille* and the *gabelle,* these indirect taxes fell almost entirely on the third estate, because the nobility and the clergy had gained exemption in the fifteenth century for the products of their demesne lands.

By the second half of the sixteenth century, the *taille,* the *gabelle,* and the *aides* had been collected regularly for so long a time, without the permission of the states general, that it had become very difficult for that body to claim the right to vote them periodically. Even the most liberal political thinkers in France were disposed to confine the authority of the states general in financial matters to the voting of *new* taxes. As the *taille* and the *gabelle* were proving elastic, this authority, if admitted, would have imposed no very great obstacle in the way of the king's efforts to raise money.

In 1596 opposition to allowing the king a free hand in matters of finance arose from another quarter. An assembly of *notables* was held at Rouen. While the third estate was always represented in these assemblies, as in the states general, its members were ordinarily not elected

4 J. J. Clamageran, *Histoire de l'impôt en France,* Paris, 1868, vol. ii, pp. 98, 495.

5 See above, p. 83.

6 Cf. E.-P. Beaulieu, *Les gabelles sous Louis XIV,* Paris, 1903, p. 30.

7 Cf. above, p. 83.

8 Clamageran, *op. cit.,* vol. ii, *passim.*

but chosen by the king. But in this particular assembly some of the magistrates and the municipal officials had been elected, and that seems to have encouraged them to be bolder than usual. The assembly claimed the right to vote the taxes for a limited period of three years, together with the right to administer a part of the national revenue. On the advice of his clever minister, Sully, Henri IV granted both requests. A council of finance (*conseil de raison*) was named to act on behalf of the assembly. It was chosen not by the members, as they had apparently intended, but by the king. Finding the financial tasks they were expected to undertake beyond their competence, the members of this council asked to be relieved of them.[9] The renunciation by the council of finance of the duties entrusted to it by the assembly of *notables* left such assemblies without substantial power in matters of taxation.

The last states general was summoned in 1614. After its dissolution the third estate of peasants, craftsmen, traders, and merchants was left without any means of challenging the king's will in financial matters. Not until the eve of the French Revolution was an effective movement started to take the control of revenue and expenditure out of the hands of the crown and confide it to a representative assembly. The French taxpayers grumbled, evaded the tax collector when they could, and made local disturbances when they felt they were treated with great unfairness. But they shouldered a burden several times heavier than the English taxpayers would tolerate.

Figures for the annual income of the French and English crowns between 1540 and 1640 tell an interesting story, particularly for those persons, so numerous in our own age, who think that human values can be measured best in statistical terms. It is necessary to remember that sixteenth-century men thought otherwise; that they did not regard statistics with as much veneration as we do. But even in that age governments had to keep track of the money they

[9] A. Esmein, *Cours élémentaire d'histoire du droit français*, 15th ed., Paris, 1925, pp. 496–7, 501–3.

collected and spent. Their methods of reckoning present many pitfalls for the unwary.[10] While it is not possible to determine the national revenue precisely, scholars have worked out reasonably reliable figures which permit us to form a rough idea of its size in the two countries during the sixteenth and seventeenth centuries.

In the last decade of Francis I's reign (1537–1546), the annual receipts of the French government were apparently about eight million *livres tournois*. At the time of Henri IV's death, in 1610, they amounted to something like thirty-five million *livres*. At the end of Louis XIII's reign, from 1636 to 1642, they seem to have averaged rather more than eighty million *livres*.[11] Even when we allow for the rapid rise in the prices of commodities,[12] the real value of the money raised by taxation had at least doubled in a hundred years.

In England, during the decade from 1537 to 1546, the ordinary revenue apparently amounted to about £200,000 sterling a year, the equivalent of some two million *livres tournois*.[13] As Henry VIII governed hardly more than a fourth as many people as Francis I, he was getting for each inhabitant of the country in ordinary revenue about as much as the French king. In the last decade of his reign he received at least as much again from the sale of church property acquired by the dissolution of the monasteries, from debasement of the coinage, and from other extra-

10 For some of the vagaries, see W. R. Scott, *The Constitution and Finance of . . . Joint-Stock Companies to 1720*, vol. iii, pp. 486–508.

11 Clamageran, *op. cit.*, vol. ii, pp. 129, 510–11; G. Hanotaux, *Histoire du Cardinal de Richelieu*, Paris, 1893, pp. 346 sqq.

12 Cf. Nef, ''Prices and Industrial Capitalism,'' in *The Economic History Review*, vol. vii, no. 2 (1937), pp. 155, 174.

13 In 1581 and 1582 the pound sterling was considered by Queen Elizabeth's ministers as equivalent to ten *livres tournois* (Conyers Read, *Mr. Secretary Walsingham and the Policy of Queen Elizabeth*, Oxford, 1925, vol. ii, p. 100 n.). Both currencies had depreciated considerably since 1540, when the relation between them was not very different (cf. A. Dieudonné, *Manuel de numismatique française*, Paris, 1916, vol. ii, *passim*, and A. E. Feaveryear, *The Pound Sterling*, Oxford, 1931).

ordinary financial expedients.[14]   Under the first two Tudors, at a time when English industrial and commercial development was probably somewhat less rapid than French, the revenue of the crown had increased much more rapidly in England than in France.[15]

The growth in the English royal revenue, which began under Henry VII, did not continue after the death of Henry VIII in 1547.   During the first decade of Elizabeth's reign, from 1559 to 1568, the receipts of the exchequer are said to have added up, in round numbers, to £270,000 a year,[16] only slightly more than the ordinary revenue during the last decade of her father's reign.   Prices had risen very rapidly in the interval, so the queen was actually receiving less ordinary revenue than her father had received.   Forty years later, in the first decade of James I's reign (1603–1612), the receipts of the exchequer apparently amounted in round numbers to £575,000 a year.[17]   Meanwhile the prices of some important commodities, such as grains, firewood, and lumber, had more than doubled.[18]   When account is taken of the change in the price level and the remarkable growth in trade and industrial output, the apparent increase in the revenue of the crown under Elizabeth is seen to be largely illusory.

James I and Charles I did not succeed in adding to it appreciably.   Heavy direct taxes, or a control over industry in the interest of the exchequer, alone might have brought them a revenue comparable to that of the French

[14] F. C. Dietz, ''Finances of Edward VI and Mary,'' *Smith College Studies in History*, vol. iii, no. 2 (1918), pp. 74 sqq.; K. Pickthorn, *Early Tudor Government, Henry VIII*, Cambridge, 1934, pp. 372–3.

[15] Dietz, *op. cit.*, p. 74; Clamageran, *op. cit.*, vol. ii, pp. 16–7, 84, 98, 129.

[16] Dietz, ''The Exchequer in Elizabeth's Reign,'' *Smith College Studies in History*, vol. viii, no. 2 (1923), pp. 80–2.   Scott gave a considerably lower figure (*op. cit.*, vol. iii, pp. 493–4), but he did not go into the subject nearly as thoroughly as Dietz has done.

[17] Dietz, ''The Receipts and Issues of the Exchequer during the Reigns of James I and Charles I,'' *Smith College Studies in History*, vol. xiii, no. 4 (1928), pp. 136–7, 140.   I have added the ''assignments by tallies'' to the ''total cash receipts''.

[18] Cf. Nef, ''Prices and Industrial Capitalism,'' pp. 166, 180.

kings. The house of commons was careful to prevent them from imposing such taxes; the common-law judges and the local magistrates did little to help them to exercise such a control. The crown was driven to expedients like the sale of royal lands, which were of no lasting help to the exchequer. On the eve of the civil war, from 1636 to 1642, the annual receipts apparently averaged something like £660,000.[19] When allowance is made for the changes in the value of money, this was hardly more than the ordinary revenue a hundred years before. It was probably equivalent to nearly nine million *livres tournois*.[20]

A comparison of the income of the French and English kings must take account, of course, of the difference in the number of people in the two countries. During the hundred years following the Reformation, the population of England and Wales seems to have grown more rapidly than that of France, but on the eve of the civil war, England and Wales had hardly more than a third as many inhabitants as the French kingdom. Even when we allow for the differences between the number of people in the two realms it is evident that, toward the end of his reign, Louis XIII was collecting much more revenue for each of his subjects than Charles I—probably between three and four times as much. Taxes in England came to something like 2s. 6d. per head compared to from 8s. to 10s. in France. Yet the material standard of living among the middle and lower orders, who bore almost the entire burden of taxation in France, was by this time probably below that in England.[21] During the hundred years from 1540 to 1640, the French kings were able to claim an increasing proportion of the national income for their exchequer, in spite of long periods of war and industrial stagnation. The proportion of the national income taken by the English kings was continually declining, while the country remained almost always at peace, the

[19] Dietz, ''Receipts and Issues of the Exchequer,'' pp. 149, 152.

[20] Since 1582, when the pound sterling was regarded as equivalent to ten *livres tournois* (see above, note 13), the *livre tournois* had depreciated considerably in value (Dieudonné, *op. cit.*, vol. ii).

[21] Cf. Nef, ''Prices and Industrial Capitalism,'' p. 178.

population increased rapidly, and the middle orders, especially the merchants and the improving landlords, grew much richer. Out of a national income hardly twice as large as that of England,[22] Louis XIII succeeded in claiming at the end of his reign a revenue nearly ten times as large as that of Charles I. It is probable that considerably more than ten per cent of all French income, as compared with some two or three per cent of all English income, was collected by the crown. The financial successes of the first Bourbons, like those of the first two Tudors, are a measure of their strength as absolute rulers. The financial disappointments of the first two Stuarts are a measure of their weakness.

During the reigns of James I and Charles I the English parliament became increasingly determined not to relinquish its right of voting all direct taxes, and also all indirect taxes on necessary commodities. At the same time, the commons were formulating a taxation policy to fit the interests of private persons with large holdings in land, in commerce, and in the rising industries. The commons generally took the position that all direct taxes on property or income were undesirable, and that no indirect taxes should be levied on necessities of life, such as bread, drink, or fuel. The only taxes the commons were willing to allow the king to increase were the duties and imposts on the import of manufactured articles and on the export of raw materials such as coal.

Like the policy of the commons limiting the power of the crown to establish industrial monopolies, its financial policy was promoted mainly by the leading merchants and improving landlords. They believed that their own interests and those of the kingdom were best served by tariffs and impositions intended not primarily to raise money for the crown, but to protect the home market for the products

[22] Gregory King estimated the ''general income'' of France in 1688 at £80,500,000 sterling and that of England at £41,700,000 (*Natural and Political Observations and Conclusions,* Geo. Chalmers, ed., London, 1804, p. 68). It is improbable that the proportions between the income of the two countries had altered greatly since 1640.

of industry and to increase the national stock of gold and silver. This policy, and that of issuing patents for labor-saving inventions, were almost the only economic policies of the crown endorsed by mercantile opinion generally in the early seventeenth century. The position of the merchants toward taxation was put clearly by one of the richest and most famous, Thomas Mun, some ten to twelve years before the civil war, in the course of his classical statement of the case for protection in foreign trade. The best way to avoid abuses in public finance, wrote Mun, is to have "the disposing of the publique treasure . . . in the power and under the discretion of many". It is true that there are some states that "cannot subsist but by the help of . . . extraordinary contributions". But this, Mun indicated, was not true of England, with its great natural wealth, and its insular position to protect it against foreign invasion. With the French king obviously in mind, he wrote that "some of the greatest Monarchs of Christendome, . . . besides those Incomes which here are termed ordinary", have added "likewise all, or the most of the other heavy Contributions". "Shall we then say, that these things are lawfull and necessary because they are used? God forbid, we know better. . . ."[23]

English merchants and improving landlords were beginning to think they had found a better guide to state policy than had been known in earlier times. They held a different view of the ends of the state from that taught by philosophers and theologians from Aristotle to Richard Hooker. Hitherto it had been taken for granted that the greatest good was to be derived from according material wealth a subordinate place in the order of goods. The merchants, the improving landlords, and the philosophers who expressed their views were coming to believe the greatest good was to be derived by allowing free play within the state to enlightened material self-interest. Were they right? The history of the last three centuries might be

[23] Thomas Mun, *England's Treasure by Forraign Trade* [1664], reprint, Oxford, 1928, pp. 63–4. The book was probably written about 1630.

fruitfully distilled into an answer to this question. This history of industry and government from 1540 to 1640 represents a small part of an attempt to answer it.

When Charles I came to the throne, it was plain that most of the powerful merchants and many of the gentry, would throw their influence against every effort he made to adopt the financial methods of the French king. The French king's taxes were no more popular in England than his religion. The policy of the commons was: no taxes at all without parliamentary consent and only such taxes with parliamentary consent as the merchants and landlords approve.

In 1629, when Charles I decided to dissolve parliament and to see what he could do to increase his revenue without the consent of the commons, he struck at the interests of the wealthiest and most powerful groups within the state. The king's halfhearted attempts to impose direct taxes, like his halfhearted attempts to establish a royal control over various industries, contributed to the growing hostility of these groups. They were determined not to part with their wealth, even if they had to destroy the king in order to keep it. "Thanks to parliamentary patriotism," Disraeli had one of his characters in *Sybil* say two centuries later, "the people of England were saved from ship-money, which money the wealthy paid, and only got in its stead [after the civil war] the customs and excise, which the poor mainly supply. Rightly was King Charles surnamed the Martyr; for he was the holocaust of direct taxation." [24]

This conflict between king and parliament on financial issues had industrial as well as commercial and agrarian origins. One of the reasons that wealthy merchants and improving landlords were unwilling to allow the king a free hand in raising money was their fear that he would use his increased authority to damage their industrial interests. His policies of enforcing industrial legislation and of participating in industrial ventures interfered with the progress of large-scale enterprise under private ownership. If

[24] *Sybil; or The Two Nations,* 1845, bk. iv, ch. vi.

he had been permitted to raise a much larger revenue, he would have been in a position to pursue both those policies more effectively. He would also have interfered with the industrial interests in another way. If direct taxes, like the *taille,* had been levied in England, they would have fallen heavily on the wealth of persons who were in a position to invest in private mines and manufacturing enterprises.

Thus the financial objectives of the crown threatened the great industrial as well as the great commercial and agrarian interests. If it was much more difficult in England than in France to impose direct taxes on wealth, this was not because the English were less able to bear these taxes than the French. It was because they were better able to bear them. Their growing wealth increased their power within the state. This wealth was derived partly from the rapid industrial progress, partly from the commercial and agrarian developments which were stimulated by this industrial progress. The early industrial revolution, by adding immensely to the property and the income of skillful merchants and improving landlords, helped to give them enough political influence to challenge the king's authority, and finally to overthrow it.

Agrarian Policy in Relation to Industry.

The agrarian policies of the English crown on the eve of the civil war were regarded by the industrial interests with hardly less distrust than the financial policies. Ever since Tudor times, the privy council had been unwilling to allow improving landlords complete freedom to squeeze the maximum yield from their lands, if they did it by ejecting some of their tenants from their holdings or by enclosing wastes and common pastures in which their tenants enjoyed ancient customary rights. The decisions of the star chamber and the court of requests were frequently favorable to the tenants.[25]

The royal agrarian policy interfered with the growth of

[25] On the whole subject, see R. H. Tawney, *The Agrarian Problem in the Sixteenth Century,* London, 1912, esp. part iii.

capitalist industry as well as with the growth of capitalist farming. Some of the expanding industries, especially mining and metallurgy and cloth making, required considerable tracts of land for sinking pits, setting up furnaces, providing water power, supplying timber for fuel and building, and pasture land for sheep and draft animals. The ancient customary rights of freeholders, copyholders, and tenants at will, both in their own holdings and in the wastes and pastures, often hindered landlords from leasing out the portions of their manors best suited for digging shafts, building dams to supply water power, or for pasturing large flocks of sheep or cattle. These rights also hindered the landlords from using the land themselves for mining, smelting, or grazing. When land was leased out or claimed directly by the landlord for industrial purposes, the tenants expected to receive compensation for the customary rights they gave up. Often it was necessary for landlords or their lessees to compound with many tenants before starting an industrial enterprise. They were always being bothered by demands for further compensation as the enterprise expanded. Thus the division of land in each manor between a large number of tenants added to the costs of industrial enterprise. That provided the landlords with a motive for ejecting peasants and enclosing land,[26] a motive which was of small importance in France because of the much slower development there of mining and metallurgy and woollen cloth making.

By attempting to protect the rights of small tenants, the English monarchs added to the annoyance felt for their economic policies by those private merchants and landed gentlemen who had important interests in country industries or in the supplies of raw materials needed to carry them on. Aided by the decisions of the common-law judges and magistrates, the house of commons set about to take ''away the will of the King from enslaving lords of manors'', as Winstanley, one of the leading reformers of the day, expressed

[26] Cf. Nef, *Rise of the British Coal Industry,* vol. i, pp. 342–3, and part iii generally.

it.   He regretted that the commons did not show the same enthusiasm to "take away the will of lords of manors from enslaving the common people"![27]   By greatly increasing the demand for land, the early industrial revolution helped to make the agrarian question a factor in bringing on the civil war.   If industrial development had been as slow in England as in France, the landlords would have had fewer motives for ejecting tenants or for enclosing considerable tracts of land.   The crown could have defended the ancient customary rights of manorial tenants against ejections and enclosures without arousing so much hostility.

[27] As quoted, E. Lipson, *The Economic History of England,* London, vol. ii, 1931, p. 416.

CHAPTER 5

GOVERNMENT INTERFERENCE AND
INDUSTRIAL PROGRESS

The classical economists and their followers have argued that most forms of government regulation of industrial enterprise, and participation in it, interfere with the progress of industry by postponing the introduction of new labor-saving devices and by holding back the growth in the volume of output. The view that government interference with economic life is almost always unfavorable to progress, has become something very like a gospel in the United States among businessmen and teachers and the large portion of the public whom they influence. How far do comparisons between French and English history from 1540 to 1640 support this view?

As stated in its crude form by the great majority of the persons who profess it, this doctrine is a dangerous half-truth. It resembles in one important respect another doctrine, that generally regarded as its antithesis, the doctrine of Karl Marx and his followers, according to which a rise in the standard of living of the masses can be brought about only through government control of all economic enterprise. Both doctrines focus the attention of statesmen and scholars upon material improvement, and encourage them to take it for granted that the only important controlling principle in education and political policy is an economic one.

A rise in the standard of living of a considerable section of mankind is always desirable, unless it is purchased by a heavy loss in the spiritual and intellectual virtues, by a heavy loss in creative art and in the standards of morality. No historian of civilization will discharge his obligations if he considers the influence of state policies upon economic development, without considering their influence and the influence of the economic development they retard or encourage upon religion, philosophy, science and art, and upon the morals of the people. These are subjects to which I hope to turn in further essays.

In the present essay I am concerned with the smaller problem of the influence of state interference upon industrial development. Even this smaller problem is not as simple as most writers make it appear, and as it seems almost always to the public in the Anglo-Saxon countries today. We must recognize that there are various kinds of state interference, and that industrial development can be measured in other ways than by the volume of production. Let us consider the influence of each of the policies that have been described in this essay upon industry in France and England. What effects had the regulation of industry by the state upon the growth and the quality of output, the introduction of machinery, and the scale of enterprise?

The Influence of Industrial Regulation.

Almost all the laws passed by both the French and English governments were of a kind likely to interfere with the growth of the industries in which success depended primarily upon the quantity of goods produced. The laws interfered especially with the progress of large industrial enterprises using machinery driven by horse or water power, staffed by a dozen or more workpeople who labored for wages away from their homes, and owned by private capitalists who took no part in the manual labor. Most of the enactments were also unfavorable to the prosperity of large enterprises where the workpeople labored in their homes for wages, on materials supplied by a capitalist or by a group of capitalists from their warehouses.

It is obvious that regulations restricting the number of printing presses in England and the number of iron mills in France were not likely to encourage a larger output of either books or iron. It is hardly less obvious that regulations making it necessary to carry the products of workshops some distance to officials to be marked, added to the costs of production. In both France and England, most of the industrial legislation imposed something of a brake on a growth in the volume of industrial output. In both, the laws specifying the kinds of tools and machinery that might be used in the various crafts make it difficult to introduce new, labor-saving inventions. In both, the laws requiring apprenticeship and limiting the number of apprentices and journeymen a master might keep, hindered any increase in the scale of industrial enterprise.

In the sixteenth and early seventeenth centuries monarchs and their advisers looked at industrial problems—as they looked at statistics—in a different way from their successors in the nineteenth and early twentieth centuries. Their objects in drafting and enforcing industrial legislation were less to facilitate industrial growth and to increase the national dividend than to strengthen the authority of the crown, to promote social justice, and to improve the quality of industrial wares. While the regulations interfered with the increase in the volume of commodities produced, they helped to maintain high standards of workmanship.

Not all the laws had these effects in the same degree. It is necessary to distinguish between various laws and especially between French and English laws. English laws were generally somewhat less unfavorable than French laws to the growth of industrial output and the increase in the size of industrial enterprise. They imposed fewer limitations on the number of apprentices and journeymen a master could employ. They interfered less with the introduction of labor-saving machinery. In France most enactments dealing with tools or machines were conservative. Many of them aimed to prevent the substitution of horse and water power for hand labor.[1] In England this was less frequently the case. The object of Queen Elizabeth in granting a monopoly of grinding malt at Bridgwater to John Court in 1587 seems at first sight progressive.[2] Court's mills were newly-installed mills turned by powerful water-driven wheels. His fellow townsmen

[1] Cf. Archives départementales du Nord (Lille), B1835, ff. 34–6.
[2] Exchequer Depositions by Commission, 9 James I, Hilary 17. See above, pp. 52–3.

complained that his monopoly eliminated a number of hand-driven malt mills, to the great distress of their owners. But the horse mills built two decades later by Robert Chute, on his own initiative and in defiance of the royal monopoly, were apparently more powerful and efficient than the royal mills. Intervention by the crown, once favorable to technological improvement, eventually became an obstacle to it.

If English laws were somewhat less unfavorable than French laws to labor-saving and industrial concentration, they also did less to protect the quality of the wares produced by maintaining high standards of skilled craftsmanship.

The differences in the character of the laws in the two countries were slight compared with the differences between the success of the French and English monarchs in enforcing them. After the accession of Henri IV in 1589 the authority of the French crown in matters of industrial regulation steadily increased. The authority of the English crown as steadily diminished. In spite of the extensive system of industrial legislation built up in England, the actual regulation of industry was very much less effective than in France between 1589 and 1640. This was particularly true in expanding industries like mining, metallurgy, salt making, and new branches of the textile manufacture, in which large-scale enterprise of various kinds was becoming common.

The Influence of Royal Participation in Industry.

The results of royal participation in industrial enterprise were similar to those of royal industrial regulation. In both countries grants of monopolies and special privileges to royal favorites interfered with the free play of economic forces. They tended to subsidize inefficient and uneconomical plants in the heavy industries.[3] Gerard Malynes, one of the ablest writers on trade in the reign of James I, pointed out to the king's ministers how artificial and wasteful it was to confine the manufacture of alum to

[3] Cf. State Papers Domestic, Eliz., vol. ccliii, no. 15.

the royal works in the North Riding of Yorkshire. In 1609 he offered "to make alum cheaper and six times better in other parts of the kingdom".[4]

The English policy of granting royal monopolies in the heavy industries was no less artificial than the French policy of establishing royal manufactures. In so far as it was successful, it probably interfered almost as much with the growth of industrial output as the French policy. But it appears to have been somewhat more favorable than French policy to the concentration of manufacturing in large plants. In alum and glass making, as in the production of gunpowder, the crown attempted to give a single enterprise the monopoly of an entire industry. The effect was to increase the amount of capital invested in one venture. The French policy of subsidizing a large number of small producers, followed in the manufacture of gunpowder, had no counterpart in England. Nor did royal officers generally take as active a part in the management of government-supported ventures as in France. The royal monopolies in England did less to interfere with the progress of private enterprise and industrial capitalism than the privileged manufacture in France.

In France the policy of government participation in industry was pushed farthest in the spheres to which it was best suited, in the fashioning by trained hand labor of the finest luxury articles and in the creation of works of art.[5] In these spheres the main purpose was not the production of large quantities of goods valuable mainly for their utility, but the development of high aesthetic standards of workmanship, and the production of objects valuable chiefly and often exclusively for their beauty. By providing a new setting for the artist in the royal workshops, the crown freed him from dependence upon the gilds. The gilds had tried to maintain good standards of workmanship. But the gild system placed the labor of the artist in the same category with that of any manual worker. As the

[4] Quoted Price, *op. cit.*, p. 84.
[5] Cf. Heckscher, *Mercantilism*, vol. i, pp. 190–2.

arts practiced under the gild system with great success in the Middle Ages were dying out in the sixteenth century, the future of the decorative arts lay outside the gilds. By fostering these arts, the French crown gave the artist a place of greater distinction and offered him an opportunity to work out special rules of his own independently of the gild regulations. The court supplied these artists with a public which cultivated good form, taste, and intelligence. That public honored the moral standards associated with Christianity (and with humanism at its best), standards which distinguish men from animals and which are indispensable to culture because they justify the expenditure of thought and labor for non-material ends. Thus royal policy helped to make France the center of European art in the age of Louis XIV. It was at least as favorable to all manual work pursued for the sake of beauty as it was harmful to the progress of heavy industry.[6]

In England the attempts at government participation in industry were confined to the manufacture of goods wanted for their utility. English painters, sculptors, tapestry weavers, makers of ceramics, and others who practiced the arts of decoration, had to get along as best they could without the help of royal workshops or subsidies. The failure of the English to develop any tolerable schools of painting, of plastic art, and of the art of design in the seventeenth century to compare with the French schools, does not suggest that freedom from government interference in these spheres was of any benefit to them. The English crown tried to follow only those features of the French policy of monopoly which were least effective and least desirable. In the face of growing opposition from the merchants and the gentry, who had stakes in mining and manufacturing, the first two Stuarts were unable to gain any such extensive control over large-scale industrial enter-

6 When French historians speak of the beneficial effects of state interference upon industry, they generally base their view on conditions in the artistic crafts (cf. Boissonnade, *Le socialisme d'état*, Paris, 1927, pp. 151 and *passim*).

prise as was secured in France by Henri IV and Louis XIII. The policy of granting industrial monopolies and privileges interfered less in England than in France with the progress of the heavy industries and the rise of industrial capitalism, partly because English policy was more favorable than French to industrial concentration, but mainly because it was much less generally applied.

The Influence of Royal Financial Policy.

The financial policies of the French kings had an influence on industrial history similar to their industrial policies. Heavy taxes on the wealth of the third estate dried up some of the springs of capital available for investment in private enterprises for mining and manufacturing. Neither the clergy nor the nobility, who escaped paying most of the taxes, were disposed to invest any considerable portion of their wealth in large industrial ventures. All over Europe the ecclesiastical foundations, with their religious objectives, were less inclined than laymen to use their funds for the development of heavy industry.[7] In France the law forbade members of the nobility to participate in most industries, under pain of losing their noble status. The only wealthy members of the third estate who gained exemption from the increasingly heavy direct taxes were those who purchased offices in the royal administration (who wore the robe and formed a lesser nobility), and those who owed their favored treatment to participation in the royal or the privileged manufactures. The former groups gave up their interests in trade and industry. The latter confined their interests to public or semi-public enterprises. In so far as the funds collected by the crown were invested in industry, they were invested in these public or semi-public enterprises. By its financial policies, the crown drained off into other channels some of the funds that might have been used in financing private capitalistic ventures.

The growth in the yield from taxes in France between 1540 and 1640 served to divert funds from the great mass

[7] Cf. Nef, *Rise of the British Coal Industry*, vol. i, pp. 134 sqq.

of the population into the royal service. This hindered the growth in the demand for industrial products whose chief value was their utility. The numerous poor in villages and towns, together with the lower middle class of small shopkeepers, artisans, and thrifty husbandmen, provided the principal market for food and fuel. They were destined to provide the principal market for the products of heavy industry. Most of the taxes fell on them. As the taxes took an increasing proportion of their earnings, the amounts they could afford to spend in buying ordinary industrial products, such as cheap furniture, bedding, clothing and hangings, window panes and common tableware, increased very slowly if at all. The increase in the demand for commodities came mainly from a small number of the wealthiest people in the kingdom, who escaped paying taxes or lived on the proceeds from them. The increase in demand came, above all, from the court and from the rich nobles who gathered about the court, or who maintained small courts of their own near Paris and in the provinces. These people, together with the royal family, on whose style of living they increasingly modeled their own, were little interested in using their surplus wealth to buy large quantities of cheap conveniences such as were in great demand in England. They laid out most of their money on beautiful buildings, and on articles of luxury and works of art needed to ornament them.

Both by their influence on investment and by their influence on demand, the financial policies of the French kings served to discourage the rapid progress of mining and heavy manufacturing, and to foster skilled craftsmanship and fine art. They promoted quality at the expense of quantity.

The inability of the early Stuarts to raise large sums by taxation, to match the revenue of the French kings, helped bring about a different distribution of wealth in England. There the royal family, the clergy, and many representatives of the old landed classes found themselves increasingly impoverished during the late sixteenth and early seventeenth centuries, in spite of the rapid growth in the national dividend. If members of the old landed classes tried to live in the same fashion as their French cousins, they soon got into debt and had to bind themselves by mortgages and other engagements to city men, who had grown rich mainly by their own skill at sharp financial practices, rather than through privileges granted by the crown. The most striking feature of English social history at the end of the sixteenth and beginning of the seventeenth centuries was the extraordinary growth in the opulence of the middle orders, the town merchants and the improving landlords who were frequently of mercantile origin. These persons were generally trained in business. They were as eager, as the old nobility and the clergy were reluctant, to invest considerable sums in mining and heavy manufacturing. No traditions or laws, like those confronting the French clergy and nobility, stood in the way of their doing so. The refusal of parliament to allow the Stuart kings to impose heavy direct taxes on wealth helped indirectly to provide the capital for the development of large privately-owned ventures in mining and manufacturing.

The financial weakness of the English crown was also a factor in bringing about a distribution of wealth that stimulated the demand for the products of such ventures. In England the style of living among the new rich in the seventeenth century differed from that of the court and the nobility in France. They were more interested in display and in material comforts than in the refinements of social intercourse, trained aesthetic judgments, and high standards of morality. In France the court and the nobility which surrounded it began to aim, under Louis XIII and even under Henri IV, at reason, judgment, refinement, and high moral standards.

The taste and the standards of the new rich in England were sometimes as execrable as they are portrayed in the plays of Massinger and later in the plays of Congreve and Wycherley. In ''A Tale of a Citizen and his Wife'', Donne gives a picture of the deterioration in character that accompanied the rise of the middle class during the early years of the seventeenth century. In speaking of the citizen, he writes,

> At last
> (To fit his element) my theame I cast
> On Tradesmens gaines; that set his tongue agoing:
> - - - - -
> He rail'd, as fray'd me; for he gave no praise,
> To any but my Lord of Essex dayes.
> Call'd those the age of action; true (quoth Hee)
> There's now as great an itch of bravery,
> And heat of taking up, but cold lay downe,
> For, put to push of pay, away they runne;
> Our onely City trades of hope now are
> Bawd, Tavern-keeper, Whore and Scrivener.

Under James I and Charles I, more persons relative to the total population than in France were in a position to buy more commodities than they needed for a bare subsistence. Taxes were light. Partly for that reason there was rather less poverty among the third estate. Together with the new rich, the shopkeepers, the substantial yeomen, and the best paid craftsmen, whose earnings were better maintained than in France against the rapidly rising prices,[8] provided a growing market for the wares turned out in increasing quantities by the heavy industries.

If the English kings had been as successful as the French in raising money from their subjects, less capital would have been available for investment in private enterprise. The demand for the products of heavy industries would have been reduced.

The difference in the direction of national economic policies in France and England, and the much more important difference in the effectiveness of royal interference in the two countries, help to account for the more rapid progress of heavy industry in England during the hundred years

8 Nef, ''Prices and Industrial Capitalism in France and England, 1540–1640,'' *Economic History Review*, vol. vii (1937), p. 178.

preceding the civil war, just as they help to account for the greater success of painting and all the decorative arts and crafts in France. How much weight should be given to government policies in determining the course of industrial development during this century? There is a temptation to regard the difference between the success of government interference in the two countries as the principal cause for the rapid growth of industrial output, the widespread adoption of labor-saving machinery, and the great progress of large-scale enterprise in England.

This temptation to discover in constitutional history the principal explanation for the early English industrial revolution must be resisted. It was after the accession of Henri IV in France in 1589, and especially after the accession of James I in England in 1603, that the differences between the effectiveness of royal interference with industry in the two countries became striking. The rapid industrial expansion in England began earlier, when the power of the monarch was greater, when the economic policies of the crown were holding back industrial progress in England almost as much as in France. The English monarchs did little or nothing to bring about an early industrial revolution. They did much to interfere with it. The disputes which arose when the privy council attempted to enforce industrial regulations, and the opposition encountered by the council in trying to maintain royal monopolies, led eventually to the collapse of the whole system of government interference. But in the late sixteenth and early seventeenth centuries the confusion and dislocation in the industrial life of the country caused by these disputes was perhaps nearly as damaging to industrial progress as the successful enforcement of the laws would have been. Such differences as existed between the extent of government interference with business in France and England, account only very partially for the great differences between the progress of heavy industry in the two countries. If Elizabeth and the first two Stuarts had been as successful as Henri IV and Louis XIII in strengthening their authority, industrial progress in England would in all probability have been somewhat slower than it was. It would still have been much more rapid than in France.

A great extension in the control of the French crown over the industrial life of the country in Henri IV's reign, did not prevent the growth of industrial output and the establishment of many new manufacturing enterprises. In spite of the increasing activity of the royal officials in enforcing all kinds of economic regulations during the twenty-five years from 1595 to 1620, this was probably the period of greatest prosperity in France during the entire century from 1540 to 1640.[9] The luxury trades and the arts benefited from the increasing support given them by the crown. Government interference under Henri IV may have hindered the expansion of the heavy industries but did not prevent it.

Again, under Louis XIV the quarter century from 1660 to 1685, when Charles II occupied the English throne, was a period of considerable industrial prosperity in France, like the quarter century from 1595 to 1620. At least one heavy industry, metallurgy, as well as almost all the luxury trades and the artistic crafts, were developing even more rapidly in France than in England. Yet the differences between government interference in the two countries were much more striking than they had ever been before the English civil war. The royal regulations in France were more numerous and better enforced; the domain of royal and privileged manufactures was extended to cover a much larger part of the country's industry. In England the privy council ceased to meddle extensively with business and stopped trying to enforce most of the industrial regulations, while the halfhearted efforts of the king to revive a few of the royal monopolies met with no success. If a let-alone government policy in economic matters were the principal basis for an expansion of heavy industry, we should expect the rate of growth of industrial output to be much more rapid in England after the Restoration than under

[9] *Ibid.*, pp. 160–1.

Elizabeth and James I. In fact it was apparently a good deal slower.

Government interference with industry is only one of many factors that help to account for the slow expansion of the heavy industries and the slow growth in the volume of production in France in the hundred years following the death of Francis I, in 1547. It would have surprised the English king's ministers nearly as much as the French king's ministers in the early seventeenth century, if they had been told that their industrial policies were harmful to national prosperity. It was chiefly English merchants, with interests in trade, mining, or manufacturing, who perceived a connection between freedom from government interference and the material improvement sought for by the "new philosophy". Francis Bacon, the greatest popularizer of that philosophy, missed the connection. He was a king's man in politics and took an active part in promoting royal monopolies. Consistency between thought and conduct was not, of course, Bacon's long suit. Macaulay has made the conflict between Bacon's intelligence and his character the leading theme of a famous essay. Bacon's espousal of the royal cause, prompted as it was partly by reasons of private advantage, may not have accorded perfectly in his own mind with his philosophical views. Yet when we consider the extraordinary growth in industrial wealth that occurred in England during Bacon's lifetime (1561–1626), when ministers of the crown did almost all they could to regulate economic life, it would not seriously reflect upon his intelligence if he had believed that a considerable measure of interference with industry by an authoritarian government was consistent with the greatest progress in material prosperity. Looking back from our vantage point in the twentieth century, we can see that such a position is not entirely correct. We can see that it is also incorrect to suppose that a considerable measure of interference with industry is incompatible with a great increase in the output of mines and heavy manufactures. The early industrial revolution in England shows that nothing any government does can prevent the rapid expansion of heavy industry, provided other factors making for such an expansion are strong enough. Governments can do something to cultivate prosperity and to determine the course of economic development, to guide it in the direction of the arts or of a multiplication in creature comforts. But they must work within the limits set by their time and place and by the objectives—spiritual, cultural, intellectual, social, and economic—of the people they govern.

CHAPTER 6

INDUSTRIAL PROGRESS AND THE FORM OF GOVERNMENT

The Rise of Constitutionalism in England.

One thing was making difficult, and even impossible, an effective control of industry by the English crown after the middle of Elizabeth's reign, after about 1580. This was the rapid expansion of large-scale enterprise and industrial output, which the government could not have prevented even if it had wanted to do so, even if ministers of the crown had realized, as most of them did not, that the remarkable prosperity of the age was helping to undermine royal authority. The attempts of these ministers to control industry in the teeth of the early industrial revolution, helped to produce an economic conflict between the Stuart kings and some of their most powerful subjects, the leading town merchants and the improving landlords. Together with the religious and the political conflicts described by Gardiner and other historians, this economic conflict, with its industrial origins, brought about the constitutional crisis of the seventeenth century. The influence of industrial upon constitutional history was more positive and probably stronger than the influence of constitutional upon industrial history.

Experience during the hundred years following the Reformation showed that Henry VII had spoken with prophetic insight about the nature of the king's prerogative, when he had expressed the intention "to keep his subjects low, because riches would only make them haughty. . . ".[1] His successors had not been able to prevent their subjects from growing rich, and the result was roughly what Henry VII had foreseen. The subjects of the English crown grew haughtier in every decade. It was much easier for the

[1] His remark was reported by the Spanish ambassador in 1498 (*Calendar of State Papers, Spanish,* 1485–1509, p. 177).

crown to enforce regulations requiring apprenticeship, limiting the scale of enterprise, and fixing the size and quality of manufactured products in a country like France, where industrial organization remained medieval and where economic changes of all kinds were taking place very slowly, than in a country like England, where the forms of industrial organization were changing rapidly and the upper middle class was rising rapidly in wealth and station. In the one case, the crown was only maintaining the conditions natural to France in that age. In the other, the crown was attempting to interfere with England's industrial destiny. It was much easier for the government to set up state-owned and state-controlled mines or manufactures in connection with new branches of industry in France, where the merchants and the gentry were mainly interested in the forms of industrial enterprise common before the Reformation, than in England, where merchants and adventurous landlords throughout the country were eager to invest their savings in collieries, blast furnaces, slitting mills, lead mines, large breweries, sugar refineries, salt-making furnaces, and small factories for the manufacture of sheet glass, gunpowder, alum, and soap. In the one case, the crown was stepping into a field that the mercantile and landed classes had little inclination to occupy. In the other, the crown was encroaching upon a field that private interests were bent on exploiting.

A century ago Macaulay explained that the fifty years preceding the English civil war were marked by "a great and progressive change . . . in the public mind", which was not in the least understood by the crown. "The Court could not see that the English people and the English government, though they might once have been well suited to each other, were suited to each other no longer; that the nation had outgrown its old institutions, was every day more uneasy under them, was pressing against them, and would soon burst through them." [2] Macaulay did not realize that industrial and economic changes played an impor-

[2] Macaulay, *Essays* ("Lord Bacon"), 1866 ed., London, vol. ii, p. 343.

tant part in producing this incompatibility. Those changes help us to understand why the wealthy subjects became unwilling to allow the crown an authority over economic development that the French kings and most other continental princes succeeded in establishing.

James I and Charles I were faced with a difficult dilemma. If they bowed to the wishes of the mercantile class and of important members of the landed gentry, if they renounced their attempts to interfere extensively with industrial development, they were bound to weaken the crown prerogative. What they would be renouncing they regarded as sovereign rights. They could not give up these rights without jeopardizing their authority in other directions. If they persisted in their attempts in the face of the growing resentment aroused among justices and sheriffs, common-law judges, municipal officials, and members of the house of commons, they ran the risk of precipitating civil war.

It cannot be said that they chose the latter course. Their industrial policies were increasingly vacillating and empirical. The civil war was the result of a large number of factors. Economic causes were perhaps of less importance than religious or political causes, though it is impossible to disentangle one of these groups of causes from another. The civil war might have occurred had there been no issues between the king and the wealthy classes over economic policy. Yet those issues undoubtedly increased the tension between the sovereign and these classes. The tension made it impossible for the king to enforce his authority in industrial matters. His inability to do so weakened his authority in other matters. The conflict with his wealthy subjects over economic issues increased the difficulties he had in raising the money that was indispensable if he was to retain the power that had gone with his office in the past. If it had not been for the increased tension resulting from the early industrial revolution, a settlement might possibly have been reached on these other matters without a clash of arms.

The early industrial revolution did much to deprive the English crown of the support from the mercantile classes and the gentry, upon whom the French kings were still able to depend. The growing wealth and power which these classes had gained, partly through their participation in industrial enterprises, fortified them in the war itself. It is possible that the king might have crushed the opposition by arms had it not been for its economic strength.

The Triumph of Royal Absolutism in France.

If the rapid industrial expansion in England facilitated the establishment of representative government, did the much slower progress of heavy industry and large-scale enterprise in France facilitate the establishment of royal absolutism? The position of the French monarchy would certainly have been stronger than that of the English monarchy even if an industrial growth similar to that in England had occurred in France. At the beginning of the sixteenth century, the states general had not the same potential power as the house of commons to thwart the king's will.[8] Although royal ordinances were usually passed (in form at least) in response to the desires of the states general, although they had to be registered by the *parlements* in order to become law in the various provinces, the French king was in a better position than the English king to legislate without consulting anyone but his own councillors. Nor was he bound in his legislative acts to the same extent as the English king by inherited customs and traditions, limiting what the crown could do. It is true that in France, as in England, there were certain fundamental, though unwritten, laws independent of the personal authority of the king and superior to it. No royal ordinance, edict, or letters patent could set these laws aside. But they were less comprehensive than in England. What distinguished them most strikingly from the traditional laws of England was that they provided no protection for the liberty or the prop-

[8] Cf. C. H. McIlwain, "Medieval Estates," in *Cambridge Medieval History*, Cambridge, 1932, vol. vii, pp. 709–14.

erty of the subject.[4] So French constitutional traditions offered less strong a bulwark against the establishment of royal absolutism than English constitutional traditions.

In French territory, as in most of the states of Germany and central Europe, the sovereign authority had played a much greater part than in England during the later Middle Ages in the development of industry. In mining and salt making particularly, princes and other overlords had shares in many of the important ventures. They maintained staffs of officials whose business it was to order the mines and salt works in the interest of their princely masters. In England industrial ventures of this kind had been rare, partly because the country had been in something of an industrial backwater. There was no such strong tradition for the sovereign to participate in large-scale industry in England as in France at the time of the Reformation. So Frenchmen found it more natural than Englishmen when their kings set about to establish royal manufactures.

At the same time the French crown was less dependent than the English crown upon the support of private local interests for the administration of its enactments. At the beginning of the sixteenth century, the French kings had at their disposal a trained and adequately paid civil service in the provinces. The English kings had only the unpaid justices of the peace and the sheriffs, who gained their living by farming, trade, or industry, and who collected rents from their tenants in the shires where they governed. Cases involving an interpretation of French ordinances, edicts, declarations, and letters patent could nearly always be brought into the royal courts, where crown judges gave the decisions. The law which guided the judges was less easily bent to sanction basic changes in industrial or commercial organization in France than in England, and was

[4] E. Glasson, *Histoire du droit et des institutions de la France*, vol. viii, Paris, 1903, p. 158; cf. Stubbs, *Constitutional History of England*, vol. i, p. 130; Ch. Petit-Dutaillis and Georges Lefebvre, *Studies and Notes Supplementary of Stubbs' Constitutional History*, Manchester, 1930, pp. 489–92.

more likely to support the crown in regulations designed to preserve the conditions of industrial organization which had prevailed before the sixteenth century. English common law was a more flexible instrument, less likely to interfere with the empirical needs of traders and private promoters of new large-scale industrial enterprises, than the customary law of northern and central France or the written Roman law of the south. During the sixteenth century the written law in France was elucidated and strengthened through the influence of a celebrated school of classical scholars and jurists, of whom Cujas was the most famous.[5] These jurists derived their view of Roman law chiefly from the Emperor Justinian's consolidation of it after centuries of autocratic government. The guiding principle behind all French law was the maintenance of precepts stated by ancient authorities in ages when capitalist industry was of little importance, and the power of sovereign princes great in the sphere in which their right to govern was admitted. The guiding principle in English common law was rather the adjustment of ancient precepts to the experiences of new ages and particular cases. French lawyers were more inclined to argue that experiences should be interpreted in the light of legal principles, than to argue, like English lawyers, that legal principles should be interpreted in the light of experiences. In the sixteenth century, when the influence of Roman law increased in a number of continental countries, the absolutist doctrines which the imperial codes had supported found little or no place in the common law of England. The common lawyers, headed by Sir Edward Coke, were the greatest champions of the liberties of the subject when James I and Charles I wanted to maintain a government hardly less despotic than that of the French kings.[6]

At the time of the Reformation the French monarchy was in a better position than the English monarchy to regulate industry and commerce and to govern in every

[5] Cf. Glasson, *op. cit.*, vol. viii, pp. 104–22.

[6] Cf. Heckscher, *op. cit.*, vol. i, pp. 277 sqq.

sphere without the participation of its subjects. If a phenomenal growth of heavy industry had occurred in France in the late sixteenth and early seventeenth centuries, as it did in England, it is improbable that France would have adopted representative government as soon as England did.

But the power of the French monarch on the eve of Louis XIV's accession, in 1643, would hardly have been as great as it was. Even ministers like Sully and Richelieu, who had a genius for administration that no English statesman of the age possessed, would have encountered much greater difficulties in carrying out their programs of government regulation and control. French absolutist traditions and French administrative skill would have had to give ground to some extent before a very rapid expansion of mining, metallurgy, and other heavy industries. Such an expansion would have involved the establishment by private adventurers of many large plants in mining and metallurgy, and of large putting-out enterprises in the woollen textile and the metallurgical finishing trades. These adventurers would have found their interests menaced by the efforts of Henri IV and Louis XIII and their great ministers to subject all private enterprise to the rigid industrial regulations of the royal enactments. They would have found their interests menaced also by the efforts of these kings to grant special privileges to all the royal manufactures and by the taxes levied on the income of all members of the third estate not in the royal service. Resistance to the arbitrary policies of the first Bourbons would have been stronger than it was, and it would have come from the bourgeoisie, the class from whom the French kings recruited most of the officials who governed the country for them and enforced their industrial policies.

The willingness of the French people to accept royal absolutism at the end of the sixteenth century has been often attributed to their desire to put an end to the insecurity caused by the religious wars of the sixties, seventies, and eighties. We now see that these wars served indirectly to strengthen the authority of the French crown in another way. Together with other factors that made France a less favorable country than England for the expansion of heavy industry, they hindered the growth of private economic interests capable of furnishing effective opposition to the policies of the Bourbons. They also hindered the growth of a philosophy of material improvement, similar to that which was developing in England, and which was helping to undermine the intellectual foundations of royal absolutism.

The success of the industrial regulations and of the attempts to raise a large revenue from industry, especially from salt making, strengthened the authority of the king in every direction. The royal manufactures drew a considerable body of workpeople, technical experts, and entrepreneurs into dependence upon the crown for their livelihood. This added to the number of subjects who served the king and who were nourished out of his revenue, already a much larger proportion of the population in France than in England. Industrial history contributed, along with constitutional traditions and along with religious, political, and administrative history, to the triumph of absolute government in France.

If the heavy industries had developed in France as strikingly as the luxury crafts and the fine arts, the interests of rich traders and landed families would have been diverted from the traditional kinds of medieval economic organization, which still occupied them in the seventeenth century. In all probability a powerful movement for constitutional government would have begun earlier than it did. This is suggested by the course of French economic history during the fifty or sixty years preceding the French revolution. During those years an expansion of heavy industry occurred in France resembling the early industrial revolution that had transformed economic conditions in England nearly two centuries before. This expansion imposed an increasing strain upon the industrial and financial policies that the French crown had been pursuing for generations. The interests of many wealthy merchants and of a few landlords in large mining and manufacturing enterprises were hampered by the industrial regulations of the crown. These merchants and landlords also objected to the royal policy of granting monopolies to royal and privileged enterprises in certain districts. They made common cause with the peasants and small shopkeepers against the royal financial policies, which interfered with the accumulation of capital, both because the heavy direct taxes fell on the wealthy members of the third estate as well as on the poor, and because the kings proved capricious debtors, who frequently resorted to debasement of the currency and even to default as methods of repudiating their engagements to their merchant creditors. The conflict between the rich bourgeoisie and the crown was precipitated by the industrial revolution in France. It played a part in the French revolution somewhat like that played by a similar conflict between wealth and the royal prerogative in the English civil war.

The form of government which emerged in England from the civil war and the revolution of 1688 was a government which represented the interests of rich merchants and improving landlords, whether whigs or tories, far better than the government of the Tudors and early Stuarts. The new government was more in harmony with the philosophy of material improvement, which made slower progress in France than in England. Modern constitutionalism owed its establishment in a measure to the rapid industrial expansion that took place in England between 1540 and 1640, and especially between 1575 and 1620. The early English industrial revolution helped prepare the way for the triumph of democracy in nineteenth-century Europe. It weakened the doctrine that human affairs are best ordered when controlled from above. It strengthened another more novel doctrine, that progress depends upon allowing free scope for individual initiative.

INDEX